The Wind and Waves of Revival

The Wind and Waves of Revival

Daniel R. Tidmore

Foreword by
Carolyn Tennant

The Wind and Waves of Revival

The Wind and Waves of Revival by Daniel R. Tidmore; foreword by Carolyn Tennant.

Edited by Lois E. Olena

Cover design and interiot layout by Uberwriters, LLC.
www.uberwriters.com

Thanks to the Flower Pentecostal Heritage Center for allowing me to display their watermarked photographs.
https://ifphc.org/

Includes bibliographical references.

ISBN: 979-8-9895495-0-4 Paperback
ISBN: 979-8-9895495-1-1 eBook

Dedication

To my wife, Bekah

Thank you for being my best friend
and for always believing in me.

Contents

Foreword

Throughout the years, I have been an avid researcher on historical revivals. I have found the accounts of how God has moved to be life-giving, keeping me spiritually fervent and hopeful. I love scrounging up old, out-of-print books and hunting down lesser-known accounts. Even though I have studied this topic in-depth, I get delighted when I run into a revival I have never heard of before, and this happens quite regularly. I taught the revivals class for years at North Central University (Minneapolis, MN) and now have the honor of teaching it in the D.Min. program at the Assemblies of God Theological Seminary of Evangel University (Springfield, MO). That is where I met Daniel Tidmore.

Daniel and Bekah's first baby, Davis, chose to arrive in the world right at revivals class time. Daniel properly stayed home for this important event and did the course by Directed Research. This book which you have before you began as his last course project. He wanted to select a few of the most important revivals and teach them to his adult Sunday school class at the church he pastors in the Ozarks.

I heartily approved this idea since I believe that most people are appallingly bereft of information regarding what the Lord has done around the world for centuries. God has come to revive His church over and over since, clearly, we keep falling backwards and need to wake up and repent. Basically, in revival we come back to life.

That is the root meaning of the word revival, in fact. The re part of this Latin root means "again" and the vival portion derives from the Latin word vivere—to live. The word revival, then, literally means "to live again." When the Church seems to be knocked down for the count, out of breath and unable to rise, God graciously chooses to come to us and shock us back to life with His paddles to the heart. I feel grateful that He does this because without it, the Church probably would not have survived into our day. Oh, how we need Him to provide a fresh wind of His Spirit!

Besides reading about revivals, I have participated in them in places like Argentina and have visited locations where revival made an impact. These have included trips to Argentina, the Hebrides islands in Scotland, a church located in the cornfields of Missouri, and the location of the Azusa Street Mission and Angelus Temple. I have preached in the little log church in Cane Ridge, Kentucky, which figured prominently in the Second Great Awakening.

What we cannot possibly accomplish on our own, God can do in a day as His very real presence visits us.

When you do things like stand in Barton Stone's pulpit on the very floor his feet touched and preach with your hand on his Bible, the reality of what God can do for us today comes alive. The history of revival shows that God uses ordinary people who in some ways are not ordinary at all because their faith in what God could accomplish was through the roof. I want my faith to be like that too. Their obedience to what God wanted them to do was exacting, and they were quick to repent. Their prayer lives were amazing; they sought the Lord's face. Let it be so for us today, Lord!

We must learn revival history because we need to be challenged. We must understand that what we cannot possibly accomplish on our own, God can do in a day as His very real presence visits us. When we hear the stories of revival, we realize what a wonderful God we serve!

I was proud enough of the revivals project that Daniel Tidmore completed for my doctoral revivals class that I recommended he take it further and make it into a book. He tested the lessons out on his own church. He worked hard on collecting accurate information, citing it, and presenting it in a concise manner. He devised questions throughout the chapter that provide for interesting discussion and soul searching.

I believe this finished product is excellent, and I highly recommend it. You can read it yourself and journal your answers to the questions. You could use it for Sunday school lessons, and if that is your choice, I suggest not hurrying through. The curriculum is perfect for Bible study groups, Wednesday night church, youth groups, and adult home studies.

I feel quite sure that when you finish, you will be excited about what God might want to do in our midst today.

The time is now for prayer and preparation regarding what I believe will be a great, last days revival! God is on the move, and He wants us to be ready to reap a harvest of souls.

Dr. Carolyn Tennant, Professor Emerita at North Central University (Minneapolis, Minnesota) and adjunct professor in the Doctor of Ministry Program at the Assemblies of God Theological Seminary of Evangel University (Springfield, Missouri).

Preface

I was fortunate to grow up in a home and church that believed in the working of the Holy Spirit. Some of my fondest memories center on times in the presence of God.

When I answered the call to ministry, I developed a love to read about the Holy Spirit. I felt I could never get enough information about what God does through the third Person of the Trinity.

For over a decade, I have become a student of revival. Whether it is through a book or listening to someone's personal stories, I have an insatiable desire to know more about what God has done.

Learning about revivals of the past builds faith that God will pour out His Spirit again. This book comes from a hunger for God's presence that continues to grow.

Introduction

Recently, we have witnessed events take place in our world that at one time would have seemed impossible. A list detailing all the changes seems redundant, for every day we are inundated with the problems and perplexities facing us. At times it can prove too much for words. Many people may feel tempted to assume that life has never been this bad. Recently, I found myself saying this and felt the Spirit correct me to realize it has never been this bad *in my lifetime.*

The subtle shift in my statement on the desperation of our society and culture caused me to wonder, *what has happened in the past when life appeared unbearable*? Thus far, humanity has not fallen off a cliff into the abyss.

When life seemed darkest, God viewed that as
an opportune time to do something new in the
hearts and lives of people.

On the contrary, I discovered that when life seemed darkest, God viewed that as an opportune time to do something new in the hearts and lives of people. While some may have noticed this detail before, it was revelatory for me. Furthermore, it was encouraging to know that when life seems the worst, God does some of His best work.

The chapters you are about to read overview what God has done in and through history. I trust that you will notice a common theme: following each generation's worst-case scenario, God arrived on the scene with a best-case scenario, which we call revival.

Join me on a journey to discover what God has done for His people in the past. Doing so should motivate our hearts and lives for what He wants to do for us.

Waves of Revival

On our honeymoon, my wife, Bekah, and I flew from St. Louis, Missouri and landed in San Francisco, California. After spending a few days in the Bay Area, we rented a car and drove south on Highway One, ending our trip in Los Angeles.

Coming from landlocked states, being near the ocean was exhilarating for us. We took turns driving, with the passenger looking out over the vast Pacific Ocean. We stopped every hour or so just to watch the ocean—more specifically, the waves rolling in to the shore.

The formation of waves is a complex scientific process. As one who likes to learn, I researched waves and discovered that each wave crashed on the shore in response to the wind that blew over the water. Though it looks as though the water moves, wind drags over the surface of the ocean, forming waves.[1]

Thinking of the wind creating waves as it blows over the water reminds me of Jesus's words to Nicodemus: "The wind blows where it wishes, and you hear the sound of it, but cannot tell where it comes from and where it goes. So is everyone who is born of the Spirit" (John 3:8).[2] As wind blows over the ocean creating waves, so does the Holy Spirit blow over the Church and God's people.

At various junctures in history, the wind of God will blow so strong over a person, church, region, or nation creating waves of the Spirit. Often these waves become known as *revival*.

The word "revival" is absent in scripture. However, we can find the word *revive* in the Old and New Testaments. The word "revive" means "to give new life, come to life, recover, or bloom again."[3]

Various authors provide insightful definitions and descriptions of revival.

"Revival means to reanimate, renew, awaken, reinvigorate, restore to new life that which is dying or dead; revival makes the church whole and happy in God again."[4]

"Revival is a work of God's Spirit among His own people ... what we call revival is simply New Testament Christianity, the saints getting back to normal."[5]

"Revival is renewed conviction of sin and repentance, followed by an intense desire to life in obedience to God. It is giving up of one's will to God in deep humility."[6]

"Revival is a work of grace. Wherever and whenever it occurs, the prime mover, the initiator and administrator of this distinctively divine activity, is revealed to be God the Holy Spirit."[7]

Throughout history, God showed himself real and powerful through the work of the Holy Spirit. Historic revivals all had one goal in mind—to point people to Jesus. When revival comes, people focus on and experience the presence of God in their church, their lives, their families, and their friends.

Often when we think of revival, we might have images of an evangelist coming to preach for a Sunday through Wednesday. God has indeed used those times to start or increase a revival in a church.

However, we cannot schedule revival. We cannot plan for revival. Instead, we must pray for revival. Revival solely comes as a work of God in response to the prayers of His people.

Can you describe a time when you personally experienced revival?

Why do we need revival?

If revival means coming back to life, we need to see what it means to be spiritually alive. One prime example of revival is the Book of Acts. God sent His Spirit, and the Church changed the world.

Just as we see waves crash on beaches and shorelines, the Spirit came into the Early Church, forever changing the course of history. They prayed consistently and depended on the power of God to work in and through them. They lived in a constant state of revival. That does not mean they did not face hardships or difficulties. Instead, they prayed in the midst of these challenges, and God continued to send new life wherever they went.

Revival comes in waves. That was the model of the Book of Acts. Just as the creation of waves is a process that includes an unseen circular motion below the surface,[8] behind the scenes and long before revival comes to a person, church, or region, there is a cycle of circular motion taking place.

Within each revival we will study in this book, we will notice a cycle:

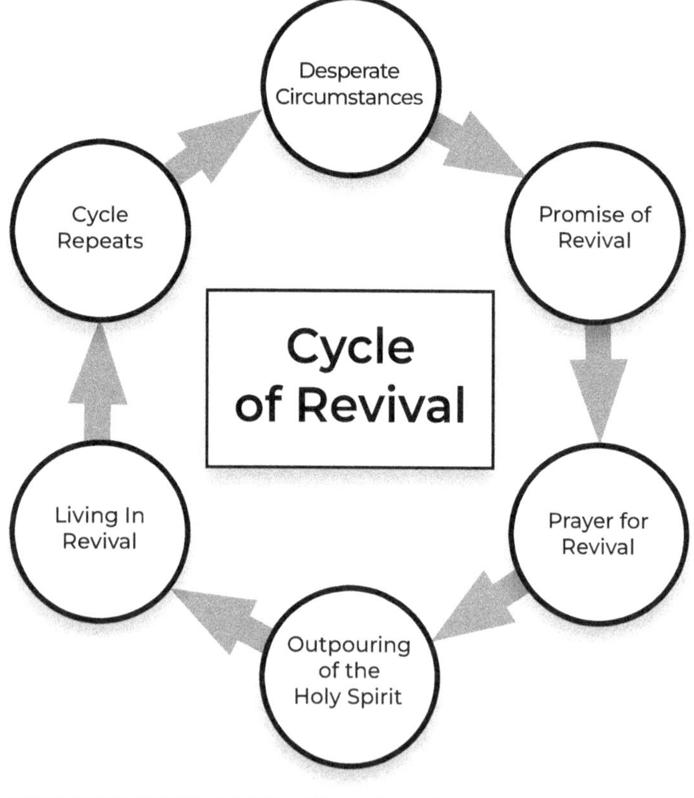

Revival begins with desperate circumstances. An individual, a church, a community, a region, or a nation will go through a time of increased immorality, decreased faithfulness to attending church, and spiritual attacks which try to stop God's people.[7]

In those moments, at times, the Spirit will speak to a group and promise revival. He also brings a Scripture or passage to their memory, rallying them to the call of revival.

A remnant will then begin to pray for revival. God will eventually respond in His way and His timing, and people will experience an outpouring of the Spirit. Then, individuals, churches, and sometimes nations will live in a season of revival. Eventually, over time, the cycle will repeat itself, bringing a new need for revival.

Where do you think our nation is in this cycle of revival?

In this book, we will look at ten revivals:

- The First Great Awakening
- The Second Great Awakening
- The 1857-59 Prayer Revival
- The Welsh Revival
- Early Pentecostal Revivals
- The Azusa Street Revival
- The Healing Revivals
- The Hebrides (*heh-brid-ees*) Revival
- The Revival in Argentina

To appreciate what God did in each revival, we need to see how the cycle of church revival began when the Holy Spirit crashed in on the Church in Luke and Acts.

Desperate Circumstances
Luke 24:36-41

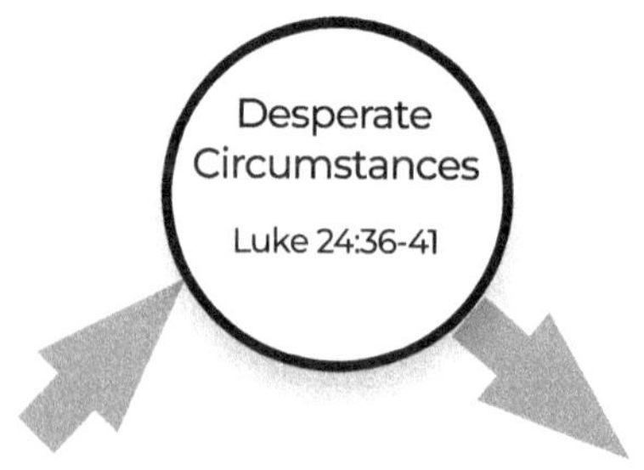

The death of Jesus was a traumatic experience for everyone involved. The disciples left everything to follow Him.

Now, their hopes and dreams for the future lay in a tomb outside of Jerusalem. Peter and John were the first of the twelve disciples to know He rose from the dead, but many of them still did not believe. As they were alone, Jesus entered and revealed Himself to them.

How would you feel if you thought Jesus was dead but then He appeared in the room with you?

Why was the death of Jesus a desperate circumstance for the disciples?

Jesus knew His disciples were terrified. They feared for their lives and their futures. Perhaps they worried whether the Jewish leaders would find and kill them too.

Do we live in desperate times?

What desperate circumstances do we see in our
world?

Promise of Revival
Luke 24:44-49

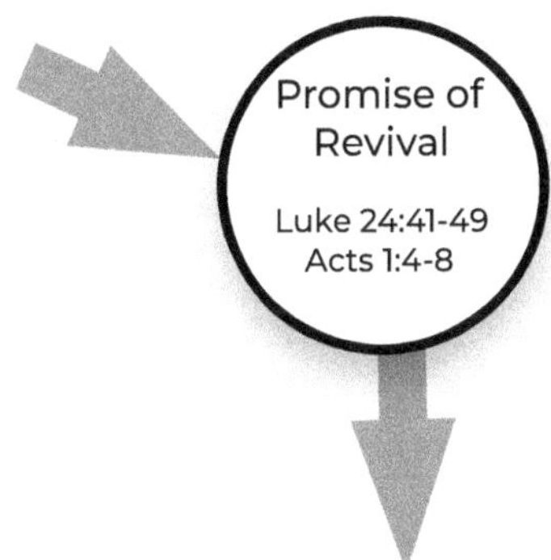

Jesus reminded His disciples of the plan of God. He showed them in Scripture why He had to die and rise from the dead. He knew He planned to redeem and save anyone who would call on Him and repent of their sins.

Yet, He needed people who would take His message to the world. Therefore, He instructed the disciples to wait for the promise of the Father in Jerusalem. He wanted them to have supernatural power.

Why was it necessary for the disciples to have
power from God?

Acts 1:4-8
Luke and Acts give one long account of the life of Christ and the workings of the Early Church. Just before Jesus

ascended to heaven, He told His followers to expect Him to baptize them in the Holy Spirit.

The disciples got distracted and wondered how Jesus was going to fix the social and political problems of the day. Jesus refocused them on spiritual matters. They needed power from the Holy Spirit.

Why is it easier to focus more on what we see in our world and less on what God has for us?

Do you think the disciples knew how Jesus would send the power of the Holy Spirit?

Prayer for Revival
Acts 1:12-14

After Jesus promised His disciples power from God, He ascended to heaven. Those who watched Him leave stood waiting. Perhaps they expected Him to return immediately.

Instead, God sent two angels to speak to them. They left the Mount of Olives and went to Jerusalem, where they met in an upper room (v. 13). As they waited, they prayed in unity for Jesus to fulfill His promise.

The twelve disciples were not alone in praying for God to send His Spirit. Mary, the mother of Jesus, some of the other women, and Jesus's brothers also sought God for the promised power.

Eventually, 120 gathered and prayed with fervor and urgency. They knew how desperate the circumstances were, so they held on to God's promise to send His Spirit.

Why do we have to pray before God can send revival?

What would have happened if they had not prayed?

Outpouring of the Holy Spirit
Acts 2:1-4

After ten days of praying, something supernatural happened.

They were united in their desire for God's Spirit. Suddenly, fire fell from heaven. Throughout Scripture, God often revealed His presence by sending fire:

- The fire of God caught Moses's attention when he was in the desert. The fire protected the Israelites on their journey to the Promised Land.
- The fire fell on the Temple when Solomon dedicated it to the Lord.
- Elijah called down fire from heaven as he sought to get Israel to return to God.

- Now, the fire fell on those waiting for God's power on the Day of Pentecost.[8]

Suddenly, they became consumed by God. They were baptized in the Holy Spirit and began to speak in tongues. Jesus fulfilled His promise to give them power.

When the power of the Spirit came on them, they came spiritually alive in a way they had not known was possible. The love, presence, and glory of God consumed every part of them.

How do you think they felt on the Day of Pentecost?

What was it like, the first time you experienced the power of the Holy Spirit?

Living in Revival
Acts 2:36-41

God had a purpose for sending His power. He gave them supernatural ability to witness. He wanted them to help others see why they needed to repent and accept Jesus as their Savior.

On the very day God sent life to the Early Church, 3,000 people came to Christ, were baptized in water, and were filled with the Holy Spirit. The Early Church then moved forward, living in the overflow of God's Spirit.

Peter made a prophetic promise: God's Spirit will come on future generations. His supernatural power was never to become merely an historical event. Rather in the future, other people would enjoy the blessings of the life-giving power of the Holy Spirit.

Acts 3:6-10

Not long after the Day of Pentecost, God used Peter and John to heal a man. From birth, the man was unable to walk, and before Peter finished praying, the man walked, leaped, and praised God.

God demonstrated His power in Peter and John for one purpose—to help others come into the kingdom of God. Peter used the opportunity to tell people to repent so God could refresh them by His Spirit.

How do you think Peter and John felt when God healed the man?

What do you think it was like to live in this type of revival?

Cycle Repeats
Acts 4:1-3

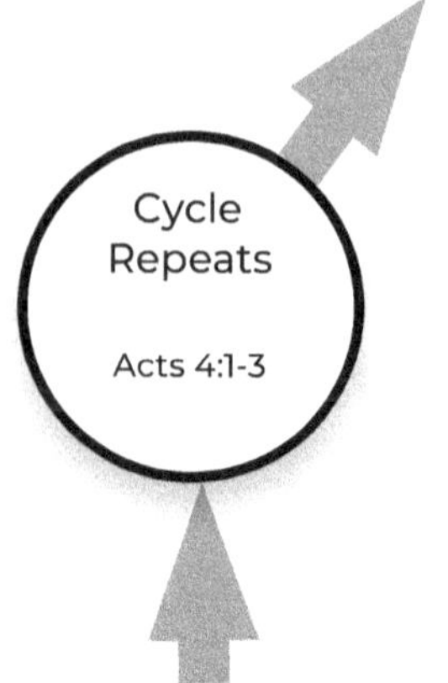

God sends revival to bring people and situations back to life. There are times when circumstances appear dead. Imagine how Peter and John felt. After they experienced God pouring out His Spirit, they turned around and faced another desperate circumstance: the Jewish leaders arrested them.

If we were to read on, we would find that the arrest and trial seemed desperate, but the Early Church held on to God's promise of supernatural power. They prayed, and God sent His Spirit to help. They then went forward, living in revival.

What do you think the Early Church did when
Peter and John were arrested?

The cycle of revival can come in a matter of days, weeks, months, years, and even decades. There are seasons when people feel as though they are in constant revival, but then they face a dry spell and become very desperate.

The emphasis is not on the circumstances but on the need to stand on God's promises and continue to pray. As we pray, when the time is right, God will pour out His Spirit, and we will enjoy living in the revival God has for us.

Application

Throughout history, God has sent revival many times. If revival means to come back to life, we need to understand what it means to be spiritually alive. The Church in Acts shows us the essence of true spiritual life.

The Early Church faced hardships. They trusted God's Word. They prayed consistently. They experienced multiple outpourings of the Holy Spirit. They lived in revival. Then they went through the cycle all over again.

Where do you think our world is in the cycle of revival?

Where do you think the Church is in the cycle of revival?

Why should we pray for revival?

What can happen to our lives, our families, our churches, and our communities when we begin to live in revival?

God wants to revive us. Whenever His people grow hungry for more of Him and pray fervently for His will, He will answer.

This book can serve as a springboard to stir our hearts to pray for God to do something special in our lives and churches.

If God answered the prayers of previous generations, why would He withhold His Spirit from us today? His track record is proven. He still saves lost people. He still fills hungry hearts. He still sends revival.

Though we cannot see it with our eyes, the wind of the Spirit is hovering and blowing. God is ready to send a wave of revival in the lives and hearts of His people.

Look at this diagram and determine where you are in the cycle of revival.

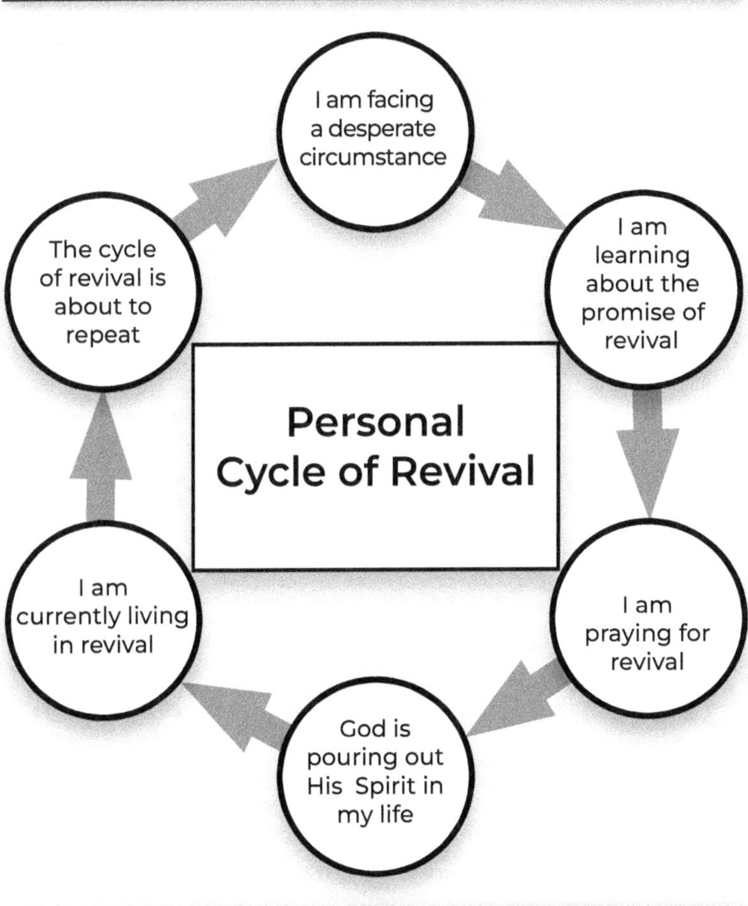

The First Great Awakening

I have not spent much time in the ocean. Even though I have visited both the Atlantic and Pacific, I have yet to get in and swim. Our family did take a trip to the Gulf of Mexico.

It was in summer, and it was hot. Even though my siblings and I were teenagers, the child in us came out as we got into our swimsuits and unapologetically played in the water. The water was refreshing and just what we needed.

We have already referred to the miracle of the crippled beggar being healed as described in Acts 3:9. The baptism in the Holy Spirit provides boldness for witness, so Peter used this opportunity to preach to the crowd that had gathered, saying, "Repent therefore and be converted, that your sins may be blotted out, so that times of refreshing may come from the presence of the Lord" (Acts 3:19). Here Peter connects repentance with refreshing experiences in God's presence.

What does repentance mean to you?

How does repentance bring spiritual refreshing?

Repentance brings a change of attitude and action from sin toward obedience to God.[9] Repentance is a vital part of our experience with God. As the winds of the Spirit blow over the life of a person trapped in sin, the individual must make a choice: repent or remain distanced from God.

When someone repents of their sins and turns to Jesus Christ as their Savior, waves of grace, mercy, and spiritual awakening flow over on them. This was a hallmark of the First Great Awakening.

Desperate Circumstances

The late 1600s and early 1700s were a period of spiritual disinterest in England and the American colonies.

While churches had people filling their pews, their ministers preached empty sermons, and the congregants had little regard for God's activity in their lives.

Problems within the church began as many ministers did not teach and actually opposed the doctrine of salvation by faith. Furthermore, many clergy were known for their drinking habits.

Because of the backslidden condition of the ministers and their parishioners, spiritual darkness and immorality consumed society. Church services declined, buildings needed repair, and worship was regularly neglected.[10]

One of the reasons for these spiritual problems stemmed from the mindset people had toward God.

Deism ruled the day. Deists believe there is a God in heaven, but He has little concern for the problems of His people. Most people tended to rationalize everything and questioned the authority of Scripture and the Virgin Birth of Christ. They were apt to doubt that God could heal or perform miracles.[11]

All in all, their spiritual condition was terrible.

How does their day compare to our times?

Why might people assume God is not interested
in their lives?

Promise of and Prayer for Revival

In the time of spiritual darkness, the Spirit winds of revival began to stir in the hearts of some people.

In the 1730s at Oxford University, a small band of students gathered to earnestly seek God to live holy. The group never grew to more than twenty-five members. Yet, every day they examined their hearts, each week they took Communion, every Wednesday they fasted, and every Friday they visited the sick.

Other students mocked them, calling the gathering "The Holy Club." Among those present were two brothers, John and Charles Wesley.[12] Little did they know the waves of revival that were soon to flow from their dedication to God.

Why would it have been hard for the Holy Club
to meet as they did?

Outpouring of the Holy Spirit

Over five hundred miles away from the Holy Club, a small group of faithful people from Moravia (modern-day Czech Republic) escaped persecution and moved to Germany. They were allowed to stay on the estate of Count von Zinzendorf.

During a time of prayer, the Moravians experienced God's presence as they received Communion and baptized people. The presence of God gripped them so strongly that every twenty-four-hours there was at least one Moravian committed to pray. Their prayer movement lasted over 100 years.[13]

The Moravians sent hundreds of missionaries with two assignments: save the lost and win the church.[14] One of these Moravian missionary evangelists, named Peter Böhler, met John Wesley, and they developed a strong friendship.[15]

At the time, Wesley lived in London, which was full of immorality. People rarely left home after dark due to crime. Every third house in London sold liquor, promising that people could get drunk for a cent or dead drunk for two and a half cents.[16]

But in such darkness, God shined his light from the Fetter Lane Moravian Chapel. Through God's leading, John Wesley and many from the Holy Club came to the chapel.

After much study of Scripture and prayer, Wesley had a special experience at Aldersgate in May 1738. His heart began to warm; he placed his trust in Christ alone for salvation and gained assurance that God had taken away his sins.[17] Throughout John Wesley's ministry,

> well-dressed, mature people suddenly cried out as if in agonies of death. Both men and women, outside and inside the church buildings, would tremble and sink to the ground. When Wesley stopped and prayed for them, they soon found peace and rejoined Christ.[18]

When God saves someone, what does He want them to do?

What are some ways God honors those who are faithful to Him?

Living in Revival

On New Year's Eve of 1738, over sixty people met at the Fetter Lane Morvian Church in London. As they brought in the New Year, the Holy Spirit began to work in a unique way. What God accomplished that night would blow over the Atlantic and deeply alter the spiritual life of the American Colonies.

One of those present was George Whitefield. Unlike John Wesley, who started life in a God-fearing home,

Whitfield was the opposite. As a boy, he was "a self-confessed liar, thief, and a gambler, addicted to filthy talk, cursing, foolishness, and fantasy."[19]

Why is God more concerned with our future
than our background when we repent?

By the time he went to Oxford, Whitefield felt God dealing with him about his lifestyle. He was exceptionally lonely and ripe for spiritual conversion. John Wesley invited him to join the Holy Club. Through study and prayer, God revealed to him that he needed to be born again.

For over a year, he wrestled with salvation. Finally, the weight of sin lifted off him, and he felt God's love and unspeakable joy.

At twenty-one, Whitefield's preaching began to startle the nation. When he delivered his first sermon, over 300 came to hear him. Wherever he preached, whether on weekdays or weekends, crowds formed to listen to the young evangelist.[20]

Crowds steadily increased, from 300 to 5,000 to 25,000. When he preached, nearly the entire congregation would weep under conviction. His preaching led him to Boston, a city with 10,000 to 12,000 citizens.

Fifteen thousand came to the city to hear him preach. One of the clergymen who rejected his message of repentance told him, "I am sorry to see you here." Whitefield replied, "So is the devil."[21]

For over thirty years, Whitefield preached across England and America. He reached thousands for Christ, never losing his passion for seeing people born again.[22]

How would it feel to see thousands of people
saved at one time?

The Wesley brothers and Whitefield were three of many people God used during the First Great Awakening. Jonathan Edwards was another man God used greatly.

Edwards spent most of each day studying and praying. He asked God to "stamp eternity on my eyeballs."[23] Churches were full of unconverted people. They attended for social and political purposes. Even kids raised in church ignored their parents and regularly walked the streets looking for trouble, partied all night, went to the bars, and lived immorally.[24]

God heard Edwards's prayer. He preached a message at his church in Northampton, Massachusetts entitled, "Sinners in the Hands of an Angry God." The men and women, who were religious, backslidden, and worldly, suddenly realized their doom.[25]

People clutched their hands onto the back of the pews, holding on, believing the ground would split open and take them to hell. Genuine conversion and repentance followed.[26]

The conviction of sin became so visible through Edwards's ministry and in the First Great Awakening. "It was not uncommon to see people collapse physically under conviction of sin as they came to see the Lord as the holy God and to recognize His right to judge their sin."[27]

For fifty years, waves of revival swept over England and the United States, bringing an awakening to people's hearts to the reality of their sin and their need to repent.

George Whitefield summarizes the feeling of the day among those touched by the Awakening: "God forbid that I should travel with anybody a quarter of an hour without speaking to them of Christ." He did just that. In his life, he spoke to over 10,000,000 people about Christ.[28]

Application

What God accomplished in the First Great Awakening was built on the foundation of prayer, humility, and a desire to save souls.[29]

Seeing how ungodly life was, did an Awakening
seem possible?

Why didn't the ungodly attitudes alter God's
desire to send an Awakening?

In a few decades, God sent an Awakening that dramatically shifted the culture of society. God wants what He did through them to impact our faith concerning what He desires to accomplish through us.

In a culture that did not believe God was interested in them, God showed His deep passion and desire for people to find salvation. They doubted the supernatural, yet God supernaturally saved them from their sins as He revealed himself.[30]

What common theme existed throughout the
First Great Awakening?

Does it seem possible for God to send an
Awakening in our own time?

Many would have doubted God could change England and America. People seemed too indifferent toward God. Immorality continued to grow. But God answered the prayers of His people.

God used the Apostle Peter, Wesley, Whitefield, and Edwards to show what is needed to experience God's refreshing. We too need to repent of our sins. When people turn from a life of sin, they show God their sincere desire to lay down their ways and follow God's plan for their lives.

The First Great Awakening began as people prayed, and multitudes started to repent. Through repentance, God gave them the assurance of their salvation. Once they enjoyed the blessings of salvation, they could not help but tell others about God's extraordinary grace.

The facts surrounding the First Great Awakening, the crowds and impact of the ministers, can grip us. However, we must focus on the foundation—prayer for repentance and prayer for the lost to repent.

The driving force of the First Great Awakening was the message of salvation through faith in Jesus Christ. As water refreshes on a hot day, repentance brings the refreshing times in God's presence.

Why does our nation need an awakening?

What can we do to see an awakening happen in our lives?

Challenge

Take time this week to examine your relationship with God. Do you categorize yourself as awakened to His plan and purpose for you? Are you walking in the joy of your salvation? Commit to pray and seek God that the blessings of salvation will become a reality in your life.

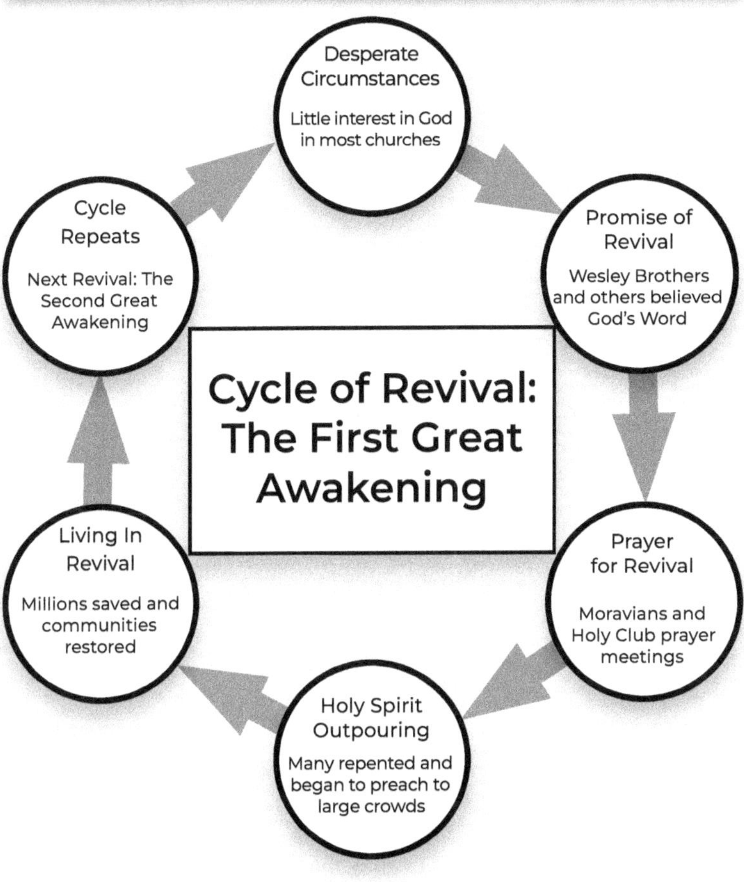
Desperate Circumstances
Little interest in God in most churches
Promise of Revival
Wesley Brothers and others believed God's Word
Cycle of Revival: The First Great Awakening
Prayer for Revival
Moravians and Holy Club prayer meetings
Cycle Repeats
Next Revival: The Second Great Awakening
Holy Spirit Outpouring
Many repented and began to preach to large crowds
Living In Revival
Millions saved and communities restored

The Second Great Awakening

My family and I spent most of our summers at Lake Eufala in Oklahoma. Most of the other kids on the beach made sandcastles. I was unique in that I created sand churches. I knew I was called to ministry and decided to get started early in building something for God.

Thankfully, the lake did not have big waves that would wreck my hard work. I had seen scenes in movies and on TV of the waves and tide from the ocean coming in and crashing into a seemingly stable sand structure.

When a sandcastle is built, the ocean may seem far away, but through the gravitational pull of the moon, eventually the waves will roll in and cover anything in their path. The dedicated sandcastle builder will have to start over again the next day.

The image of the waves receding from the shore reminded me of the life of King David. After serving God diligently, eventually his life got further from God. He began to do the unthinkable, living a life consumed with sin and guilt.

Not until God sent the prophet, Nathan, who confronted David of his sinful condition, did David promptly return to God and pray,

> Create in me a clean heart, O God, And renew a steadfast spirit within me. Do not cast me away from Your presence, And do not take Your Holy Spirit from me. Restore to me the joy of Your salvation, And uphold me by Your generous Spirit. Then I will teach transgressors Your ways, And sinners shall be converted to You (Psalms 51:10-13).

David's sincere desire was to live in God's presence and in fellowship with the Holy Spirit.

What happens when we distance ourselves from
God's presence?

Desperate Circumstances

After the remarkable awakening that occurred under the ministry of John Wesley, George Whitefield, and Jonathan Edwards, slowly, churches begin to fall back asleep. The eyes of America were on the Revolutionary War.

Once the war was over, people settled into their new lifestyle as an independent and free nation. While the Church's influence decreased in society, Satan reached his hand into people's lives.

Much of the world entered the Age of Enlightenment. People became more skeptical about God and His interest in people. They rejected God's ability to reveal himself to humanity and denied His supernatural power.[31]

Thomas Jefferson had what was known as the *Jefferson Bible.* He kept the life of Jesus, but eliminated any mention of miracles, healings, or divine intervention.[32]

Can we pick and choose which Scriptures we
will live by? Why or why not?

The Age of Enlightenment gripped universities and Bible colleges. Christian students became the minority and met secretly to avoid persecution from those who denied God.[33] Because the colleges trained clergy, humanism and denial of biblical revelation became common in churches, through the lack of belief of their pastors.[34]

The attitude of spiritual disinterest created many moral problems for society. The days of communities coming together to worship God became a thing of the past. Therefore, drunkenness was epidemic. Out of a population of 5,000,000, there were 300,000 confirmed drunkards, killing 15,000 each year in the United States. Profanity was common, and people robbed banks daily.

Even the Chief Justice of the Supreme Court, John Marshall, wrote that the church "was too far gone to ever be redeemed."[35]

> How do you think God feels when He sees
> people living in such immorality?

> What is His answer to the sins of society?

Promise of and Prayer of Revival

Though society drifted deeper and deeper in sin, God stirred people's hearts to pray. What God did in the United States through the first half of the 1800s has become known as the Second Great Awakening.

God called people who would go to the countryside, the colleges, and the cities to lead people to repentance.[36] The awakening happened on two fronts—in the wild West and in cities and colleges.

> How would it feel not to have a local church?

With the purchase of the Louisiana Territory, many families moved west to create a new life with more land and opportunity. However, there were few churches. Therefore, circuit-riding preachers would travel two hundred to five hundred miles per year, preaching in thirty to fifty different locations.[37]

They established what became known as camp meetings. People came from hundreds of miles away. They stayed in tents and enjoyed church services out in the open.[38]

One camp meeting happened in Cane Ridge, Kentucky.

Presbyterian minister, Barton Stone, scheduled services from Friday to Monday with Communion offered. He expected a large crowd, so he planned to have the service outside.[39] The size of the crowd astonished everyone, estimating twenty thousand people coming from many neighboring states.[40]

What would make someone travel hundreds of
miles to be in a church service?

Living in Revival

Nothing exceptional happened until Monday. At the end of the service, one woman finally gave way to what she felt. She sought God for assurance of her salvation. When she knew she was saved, she began to shout loudly.

The congregation sat, and many silently wept. Another pastor sat and began to tremble under the power of God.[41] Revival came to the frontier.

Because of the large crowd, people broke off in sections as local pastors preached from tree stumps and the backs of wagons. Throughout the camp, people were struck under conviction. "Sometimes they would fall by the hundreds all at once. They hit the ground like trees felled by one swing with a powerful axe."[42]

Many rejoiced for what God did, but some mocked. One man found the emotions of the camp meeting humorous and joked about people's responses. The more he made fun of them, the more uncomfortable he became. He finally ran into the woods to get away from the church service. He did not get far before he was struck to the ground. He laid there until he fully submitted his life to God.[43]

The cry of prayer from many people after the camp meeting was, "Lord, make it like Cane Ridge."[44] God heard, and similar outpourings occurred in the West. Shouting and emotional praise became common in churches on the frontier. People would clap their hands, run around in joy, and occasionally leap as everyone prayed.[45]

Why do you think they showed such emotions?

How does God touch our emotions when we experience His presence?

Preaching on sin and repentance became common. One circuit-riding preaching, Peter Cartwright, had an unusual experience. One Saturday, he stayed at an inn. After dinner, people would go to the floor to dance.

A beautiful young woman curtsied and asked him to dance. He agreed and led her to the middle of the floor. Then he told everyone in a loud voice, "I do not undertake any matter of importance without first asking the blessing of God on it." Taking the woman's hand, he said, "Let us pray."

He prayed loud and long. Some people left, but many joined him, kneeling on the floor. After prayer, he preached a sermon. He continued until it was time to go to bed. The next day, he preached at the inn. Thirty-two people got saved, and they formed a church. The landlord of the inn became the leader of the congregation.[46]

God was awakening people's hearts to repentance and conversion on the frontier, but He did not forget about the colleges or cities.

One of the most influential ministers of the Second Great Awakening was Charles Finney. He was an educated lawyer in Adams, New York, who had not heard gospel preaching by the age of twenty-six.

Some church members invited him to a prayer meeting. He refused their invitation, knowing he was a sinner. He then told them, "You have been praying for a revival of religion ever since I have been in Adams, yet you have it not."[47]

Something gripped Finney, though, and he went to the woods to pray alone. He had a supernatural conversion. That evening he had a vision that he fell weeping at the feet of Jesus. The Holy Spirit came upon him, and he began witnessing to others about Christ.

God used Finney, who once rallied against Christianity, to become an evangelist, beginning in New York. When he preached his first message, someone in the crowd came with a pistol, planning to shoot the speaker that evening. That man fell to the floor under the power of God and was saved.[48]

Everywhere Finney went, God did something supernatural. Finney went to the town of Rome, New York. Revival broke out after the third service and went on for twenty days. A sheriff from Utica, New York, twenty miles from Rome, mocked when he heard about the revival.

That sheriff had to go to Rome on business. When he was within one mile of the city, the presence of God shook him.

Everywhere he went, people could hardly speak because of their awe of God's presence.

The sheriff returned home to Utica, where he gave his life to Jesus. When he arrived, he began to pray for revival, and God answered.

Over 500 people were saved in Utica. The city developed a reputation of being all about God. Wherever people went, someone was witnessing and telling others about Jesus.[49]

One of Finney's most notable revivals took place in Rochester, New York. He stayed there for six months, preaching in the churches. It was there that he called people to the front to receive salvation or prayer, creating what we know as the altar call. Many people—both poor and wealthy—responded.

In one school, many students came under conviction and met together to pray for two weeks. Finally, the principal, who did not believe in what God was doing, went to the room. He found students weeping over their sins in their classrooms. He contacted Finney, who came to the school. Every student and the principal got saved. More than forty of these students became missionaries.[50]

What has God done for your life during times at an altar?

What would a revival like this do for your community?

The prosecuting attorney of Rochester was also converted. The population of the town grew by two-thirds, but crime decreased by two-thirds.[51] Out of a population of ten thousand, at least eight hundred were saved in this revival.[52]

Finney's Rochester revival became a pattern of what God did in other communities.[53] News of what God had accomplished in Rochester sparked a revival in fifteen hundred towns in New England. It is estimated that one hundred thousand people were saved because of what God did in Rochester.[54]

Application

What God revealed at Cane Ridge and through Charles Finney barely scratches the surface of what He did during the Second Great Awakening. Throughout the nation, people who were cold and distant toward God came to find Him as their Savior.

The lack of faith of the masses did not thwart the prayers of the few. God used people from all backgrounds and levels of education in this particular awakening. Dr. Timothy Dwight is an example of someone who "refused to believe the pursuit of knowledge was in any way hindered by faith in God."[55]

During his tenure as president of Yale, the awakening touched the campus, and a third of the student body converted to Christ. From the campuses, God's Spirit moved west to Cane Ridge.[56]

The message of some at the Cane Ridge Revival was simple: "whoever preaches the kingdom of heaven, must preach deliverance from all sin: for where sin is, there can be no heaven."[57]

The message of the Second Great Awakening may have been new for that generation, but the concept of repentance is ancient. Scripture lays out a promise: with repentance comes revival.

Those in the Second Great Awakening received clean hearts, time in God's presence, and restored joy. They taught people the way of salvation, and many sinners were converted.

Charles Finney preached, "revival is renewed conviction of sin and repentance, followed by an intense desire to live in obedience to God. It is giving up one's will to God in deep humility."[58]

For some, it may have seemed that the waves of revivals receded after the First Great Awakening, but the Spirit of God began to blow on the hearts of people, and revival soon followed.

Do you think the Church as well as society in
general needs to repent? If so, why?

Do we need an awakening? If so, why?

Challenge

Perhaps you have had encounters with God in the past. The Second Great Awakening reminds us that God can revisit nations and churches. Ask Him to come near to you again. Take time to repent and call on Him. If you have someone on your heart who is not where they need to be with God, pray for the Lord to restore the joy they had when they walked with fellowship with Him.

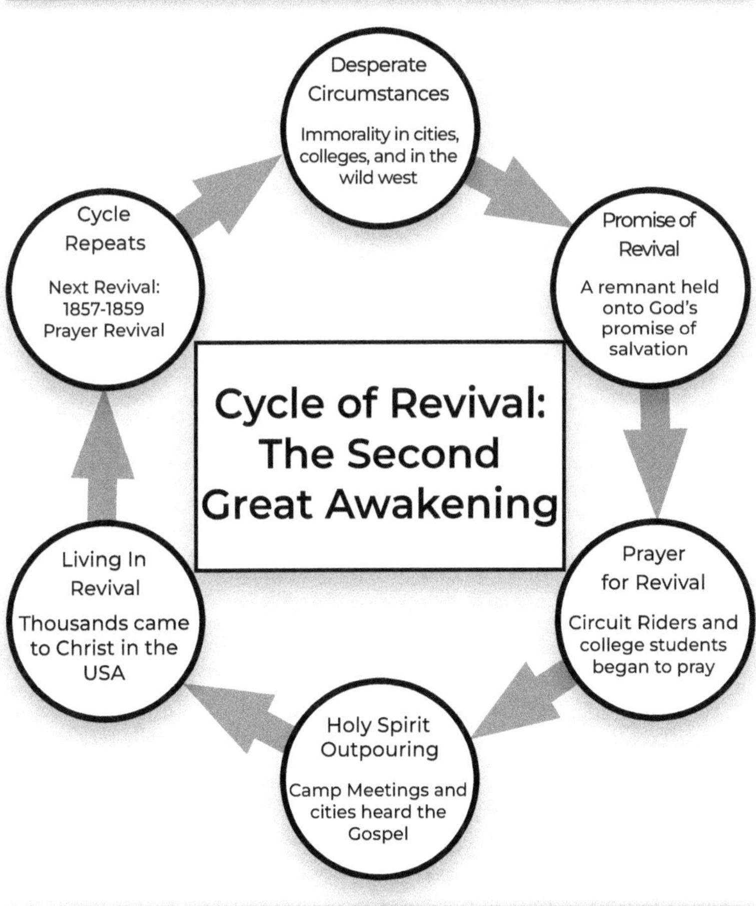

The 1857-1859 Prayer Revival

I am not the best swimmer, but I love jumping off the diving board or from an anchored boat into a lake or river. I am not a proficient diver because I still have to plug my nose whenever I jump. I realize I look somewhat absurd, but the joy of plunging into the deep end outweighs the opinions of others.

I have found that when I wear a life jacket, swimming requires much less effort. I always prefer something else to keep me afloat in the water. Whatever flotation device I use, I thoroughly enjoy coming to the surface and flowing with the waves as the wind blows over the water.

Just as a life preserver or innertube keeps me afloat, prayer keeps us flowing with the currents of life. The Early Church discovered this in the Book of Acts.

The Apostles Peter and John were the first leaders to face an arrest and trial for simply doing what God had called them to do—extend His Kingdom. After Peter and John prayed for the sick man at the Beautiful Gate, religious leaders arrested them and threatened them to not keep preaching or teaching about Jesus.

I love their response: "But Peter and John answered and said to them, 'Whether it is right in the sight of God to listen to you more than to God, you judge. For we cannot but speak the things which we have seen and heard'" (Acts 4:19-20). These apostles dove headfirst into the will of God for their lives.

They left the trial acquitted for lack of evidence. Joining the other believers, they knew they needed God's help. Therefore, they began to pray, asking God for boldness and for signs and wonders to follow their lives.

God listened! "And when they had prayed, the place where they were assembled together was shaken; and they were all filled with the Holy Spirit, and they spoke the word of God with boldness" (Acts 4:31). The Holy Spirit enabled the Church to flow where the wind of the Spirit took them. As they continued to pray, waves of supernatural power overtook their walk with Christ.

How has prayer helped your life?

Why does God desire that we pray?

Desperate Circumstances

The United States was fortunate to experience two Great

Awakenings. However, by the 1850s, many people had stopped focusing on God and instead headed to California to make it rich in the Gold Rush. Westward expansion took the United States from coast to coast.[59]

As the nation became more prosperous, greed and gambling became prominent. A renewed interest in the occult, sorcery and evil supernatural influence became evident. Immorality in relationships took the place of purity. Corruption became the norm in business and politics.[60]

The nation was more divided than ever. The issue of slavery was on everyone's minds. People could tell that war was near.

God allowed the nation to plunge into darkness for a while, then a financial crisis hit. The panic of 1857 caught Wall Street by surprise. Many businesses, merchants, and suppliers filed for bankruptcy, leading to high unemployment.[61]

One city hit particularly hard by the financial collapse was New York City. Thirty thousand men sat unemployed and idle in the city.[62]

To solve the problems of society, God stirred the heart of one man to seek the Lord. Through his desire to communicate with God, the Lord sent a revival that spread through the United States, Europe, and worldwide.

The unique part of the 1857-59 prayer revival has to do with who God used. In other awakenings or revivals, God used influential evangelists or churches. Yet, in this revival, God started with just a man who possessed a burden to pray.

Why do you think God chose to send another
revival to a nation that already had two
awakenings?

What does it mean to you that God used one
man to help bring revival?

Promise of and Prayer for Revival

In the 1850s, New York continued to grow into a bigger
city. As a result, many people moved from the city, causing
the downtown churches to suffer from low attendance. One
church, the Old Dutch North Church on Fulton Street, nearly
closed its doors.[63]

The body of believers had one more option: hire a lay
missionary to help the struggling congregation. They invited
forty-six-year-old Jeremiah C. Lanphier to come and help.[64]
Initially, he knocked on doors to invite people to church, but
few seemed interested.

Why is it discouraging when people are not
interested in what we have to say
about the Lord?

What should we do when people ignore our
invitation to know more about God?

He knew the problems that surrounded the Old Dutch
Church. Because of the economic collapse, there was often

violence and riots. As he walked the streets, he had an idea. What would happen if he opened the church from 12:00-1:00 p.m. for an hour of prayer? He decided to invite local businessmen.

He designed the prayer meeting so people could come for as short as five minutes to the entire hour.[65] The day arrived—September 23, 1857—for the first prayer meeting.

He placed a sign outside that read, "Prayer Meeting from 12 to 1 o'clock—Stop 5, 10, or 20 minutes, or the whole hour, as your time admits."[66] At noon, he was the only person there. For thirty minutes, he waited alone.

How would you have felt if you were the only
one to come to a prayer meeting?

Eventually, at 12:30 p.m., six men arrived. The next week they had twenty. The following week they had forty. In the fourth week, over 100 men came to pray.[67]

Finally, on the same day as the Panic of 1857 when the stock market crashed, people began to catch onto the importance of prayer. Eventually, the crowd grew to more than three thousand in attendance at various churches. Doctors, lawyers, bankers, mechanics, and messenger boys were in attendance. Shops put up signs on their doors: "Closed. Gone to the Prayer Meeting."[68]

They structured the meetings around prayer. The focus was not to hear preaching, but to spend time seeking the Lord. People explained, "We've heard instruction until we are hardened; it is time for us to pray."[69]

Why should we long to pray as much as we
desire to hear preaching?

Outpouring of the Holy Spirit

As they prayed, God responded. At one prayer meeting, a man came with plans to murder a woman and take his own life. As he listened to people exhort and pray, he cried out, "Oh! What shall I do to be saved?" One prayer request came from a father: "I wish to ask the prayers of this meeting for two sons and a daughter." Then he sat down and burst into tears, laying his head down and sobbing like a broken-hearted child.[70]

Similar meetings began in New York City. Local papers from the day estimate that at least sixty-one thousand people attended prayer within the city each day.[71] Some reports state that during the prayer meetings, at least ten thousand people were getting saved each week.

The New York Times reported on March 20, 1858, "The great wave of religious excitement ... now sweeping over this nation, is one of the most remarkable movements since the Reformation. ... It is most impressive to think that over this great land tens and fifties of thousands of men and women are asking themselves at this time in a simple, serious way, the greatest question that can ever come before the human mind: 'What shall we do to be saved from sin?'"[72]

Have you ever personally experienced a revival
that got national attention?

Living In Revival

Eventually, the prayer meeting movement spread throughout the nation. Major cities around the United States had a similar story and testimonies as the Fulton Street Prayer Meeting. Even businesses caught onto the importance of prayer. They would blow the lunch whistle at 11:55 a.m. to give people time to get to the nearest church to pray. They would then wait to blow the whistle until 1:05 pm to provide them with time to return.[73]

These national prayer meetings produced powerful testimonies.

One of the original six from the Fulton Street prayer meeting was from Philadelphia. He started a prayer meeting in his city. Initially, he had forty come and then sixty. He longed to see a similar prayer movement take place in his hometown.

Then, suddenly, 300 came, then 2,500 came. Finally, they set up a tent, and within four months, one hundred-fifty thousand people had come to pray in the tent.[74]

In Kalamazoo, Michigan, someone read a written request, "A praying wife requests the prayers of this meeting for her unconverted husband." Five different men stood and acknowledged, "I am that man." The salvation of those five men led to a revival that saw 500 conversions.[75]

The United States entered a new realm of prayer and faith. Even President Franklin Pierce attended many of the noon prayer meetings. About fifty thousand people were converted each week. Some estimate that two million souls were born again during the revival. The Holy Spirit covered the country. Even those traveling to the nation by boat could sense something unique about what God had done in the United States.[76]

But God did not keep the fires of revival in the United States only. The prayer revival spread to Ireland, Wales, and Britain. In Ulster, Ireland, hundreds of prayer meetings began.

The results were nothing short of miraculous. The horse races went from drawing twelve thousand gamblers to a small crowd of 500. A whiskey distillery in Belfast, Ireland, had to go up for auction because of a lack of business. Local pubs were closed as nearly ten percent of the population came to Christ.[77]

Prayer meetings broke out in kitchens, barns, schoolhouses, churches, fields, and on the side of the road. People would stop their farm work to get to prayer meetings and church services.

As a result, drunkenness, swearing, and fighting decreased. Many people carried their Bibles with them and would take breaks to stop and read the Word. Even one country fair ended in a prayer meeting with five thousand people present.[78]

How do you think the revival affected their community?

What would a revival like this do for our community?

On the island of Wales, the revival was also evident, especially among children. They began to pray and sing for hours at each other's homes and schools. Three young men got under conviction in a quarry and began to weep. The next day after lunch, all 500 men of the quarry met on the hill to pray. They sobbed as they sought God.[79]

A spirit of prayer swept across much of the world. Thousands were touched, and millions came to the Lord. God heard the prayers of one man who wanted to see heaven come down in his church.

Application

Society has faced many changes over the years. However, one thing remains constant; when people dive headfirst into prayer, God responds. The Early Church endured many trials and hardships, but they remained faithful and consistent to pray.

Jeremiah C. Lanphier lived in a tumultuous time. It could have been easy for him to remain silent and allow his surroundings to discourage him. Instead, he depended on God, knowing that prayer changes situations.

What should we do when we face hardships?

What happens if we quit praying when times get
difficult?

Lanphier could have allowed the size of the crowd and
the lack of interest to discourage him. Instead, prayer became
the life sustaining force that helped this group flow with the
opportunities and challenges that lay before them.

Whether through the prayers of the Early Church, those
of people in the 1850s, or any time, trusting God against all
opposition works. God can shake our lives and give us a
fresh outpouring of His Spirit.

When people pray, God supernaturally intervenes
under challenging situations. He also accepts many people
who called on Him for salvation. Our prayers serve as a life
preserver to help us flow where the Spirit takes us, regardless
of what we face.

What can God do through our prayers?

Does God still answer prayers
as He did in the 1850s?

Challenge

Consider taking your lunch hour for the next week and spend time in prayer. Think about the state of your life, community, and nation, and listen to God as you pour your heart out to Him. When you pray, expect God to answer.

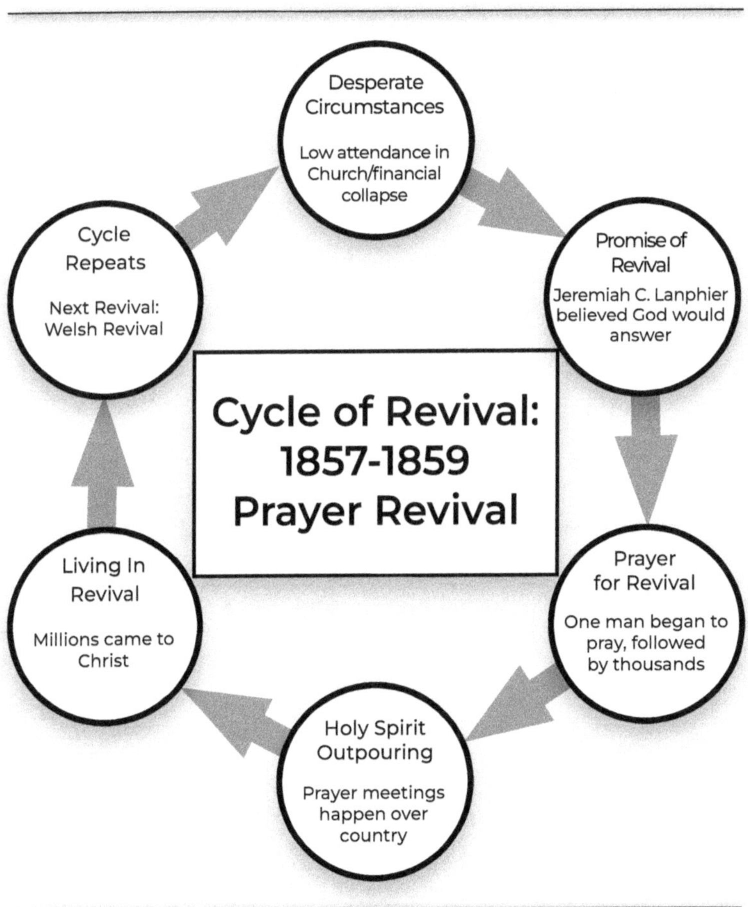

The Welsh Revival

Even though my family spent most of our summers at camping at the lake, it took me a long time to like the water. For much of my childhood I was afraid of swimming. If I had to go in past my waist, I would have a meltdown that reverberated through the entire campsite.

It did not matter how much my parents explained the way a lifejacket worked. Every day I would put it on and determine to go in over my head and let the lifejacket do its job, but every day I would turn around and go where I felt safe.

Eventually, I ventured into the water over my head and enjoyed playing with my siblings and friends. It surprised me just how much I loved the water and what I had missed for the years I refused to go with the flow.

Revival is like my fear of water. Until someone experiences a genuine outpouring of the Holy Spirit, they do not know what they are missing.

The Prophet Isaiah longed for God to do something unprecedented. He cried out to God:

Oh, that you would burst from the heavens and come down! How the mountains would quake in your presence! As fire causes wood to burn and water to boil, your coming would make the nations tremble. Then your enemies would learn the reason for your fame! When you came down long ago, you did awesome deeds beyond our highest expectations. And oh, how the mountains quaked! For since the world began, no ear has heard and no eye has seen a God like you, who works for those who wait for him! (Isaiah 64:1-3, NLT).

Isaiah's prayer is sincere and provides an excellent description of revival. There are moments in history when it seems that God bursts from heaven and does something awesome—something that goes beyond what anyone could expect.

Can you describe a time when God exceeded
your expectations?

Many were radically changed during the 1857-59 prayer revival that took the United States and much of Europe by storm. Those who lived through the prayer revival were forever marked by the ability of God to shake a nation, region, and community.

William T. Snead, a Christian who worked as a magazine editor, shared his experience with the prayer revival. He called himself a "child of the Revival."[80] In 1861, he went to a Christian boarding school in Wales.

Not everyone at the school was a follower of Christ. Therefore, some of the students gathered together to have prayer meetings for the salvation of their peers. Snead attended, not because he desired to pray but because a friend had asked him to go.

All the boys at the prayer meeting were under fourteen. The schoolmasters did not encourage the prayer meetings either. One of them disliked the meeting and insulted the boys who attended.

After a week or two of prayer, something changed at the school. Conviction fell upon the campus. The principal dismissed evening classes to allow for all-night prayer meetings.

Eventually, only six of the students stayed away from what God did. The boys prayed for those six, and some confessed their sins and joined the prayer movement.

The prayer meeting continued every evening for two years. The boys had a burden for the lost, even writing their family members begging them to confess their sins and turn to Christ.[81]

How does revival change a child's life?

Would it be possible for a revival like that to
happen twice in an individual's lifetime?

Snead kept his experience to himself. Many people asked him to share what God did when he was a child. He chose to keep it private for over forty years.[82] However, something happened in Wales in 1904.

Wales is about the size of New Jersey. Yet God visited this tiny region as the wind of the Spirit blew upon their lives. Eventually, waves of revival flowed from Wales and saturated other parts of the world.

Snead shared, "I hope my reader will understand how it is that I, being a child of the Revival of 1858 and 1861, should hail with exceeding great joy the reappearance of Revival in 1904."[83]

How would we feel to experience revival twice
in our lives?

Desperate Circumstances

The hunger for God to do something in Wales started around 1890. A twelve-year-old boy named Evan Roberts went to work at a coal mine. By the age of thirteen, he longed for God to fill him with the Holy Spirit and to send revival to Wales.[84]

Wales needed revival. Christians watched as worldliness took hold of people. Many went to church, but there was little to no spiritual life in congregations. One church leader described the spiritual condition: "while the church sleeps, the enemy busily sows tares among the wheat. Nothing short of an outpouring of the Spirit from on high will uproot them and save our land from becoming prey to atheism and ungodliness."[85]

Promise of and Prayer for Revival

Wales needed someone who would pray for God to pour out His Spirit. Roberts attended a revival service, where the evangelist prayed, "Lord, bend us."[86] The Holy Spirit spoke to Roberts: "That is what you need." Roberts began to pray and cry out to God, "Lord, bend me."[87]

God heard Roberts's cry. He became burdened with the decay of people's faith. Atheism began to take root, and evil became common. People drank, wasted time gambling, and enjoyed living in immorality.[88]

Although God used Roberts to help Wales, he was not the cause of the revival. God heard the remnant of people who prayed for an outpouring of the Spirit. Roberts was the answer to their prayers.[89]

What do you think Evan Roberts meant when he prayed, "Lord, bend me?"

Why are humility and dedication to God necessary for revival?

In 1903, before the great revival started, four young Welshmen began to pray every night for revival. The group steadily grew. For six months, they sought God to send His Spirit.[90]

The more Roberts prayed for God to bend him, the closer he was to being filled with the Spirit. Finally, after thirteen years, he had assurance that Jesus had filled him with the Spirit. With newfound power, Roberts "felt ablaze with a desire to go through the length and breadth of Wales to tell of the Savior."[91]

Many people were unsaved, yet Roberts remained undeterred in his desire for God to save 100,000 people. At the time, the population of Wales was 2,012,876 people.[92] If

God would answer his prayer, nearly five percent of Wales would come to Christ. The Lord confirmed his prayer with multiple visions.

Roberts had one vision of the schoolroom in his village. He saw his friends sitting there. God spoke to him: "Go and speak to these people." He said yes to God, and the vision vanished.[93]

The next night, he asked his pastor for permission to meet with the youth. Seventeen youth attended. "Very little happened in the first service. On Tuesday, more young people came, and a few of them confessed their sins and accepted Christ as their Savior."[94]

Outpouring of the Holy Spirit

Each night God's presence increased. When the first week of the revival ended on Sunday evening, by midnight the entire congregation wept and prayed. Eventually, they began sing, praise, and lay prostrate on the floor. People got home by 3:15 a.m. Another service even lasted until 6:00 a.m. [95]

Roberts had a simple message:

1. Confess all past and present sins.
2. Ask God to remove anything doubtful or [any] questionable actions.
3. Obey the prompting of the Holy Spirit.
4. Confess Christ openly and publicly.[96]

These four instructions governed the revival. Roberts did little preaching. Instead, people would gather, and the Spirit would begin to work. On the second week of the revival, the crowds grew larger. They had to move to a new building. Coal miners would run to the church in their work clothes, worried they might not find a seat in the building.[97]

Living in Revival

For over a year, revival shook Wales to its core. Bookshops ran out of Bibles. Homes experienced joy and singing. The coal miners became changed men. Even the most hardened sinners came to Christ in the meetings.[98]

One unique aspect of the Welsh Revival was the emphasis on singing and worship. The services did not have instruments, only multitudes of voices raised in worship. Seventy-five percent of the meeting was signing. However, there were no songbooks. People would pray. Someone would stand to testify. Another would begin a song.

If anyone got out of line or carried away, someone would start to sing. The people would join as loud as they could to worship the Lord.[99]

Why should worship play an important part in a service?

God responds when people worship. As they sang, the Spirit of God would stir the church and then reach the community. Rough coal miners would feel drawn to the meetings. Those who resisted would feel convicted until they left work to get to the church. Strong men would weep as they repented. Women and children would hum the music from the revival through the day.[100]

Annie "Florrie" Davis was among those drastically changed in the revival. Roberts invited her to join his evangelistic team. She would sing, preach, testify, and prophesy in the meetings.[101]

The London Times reported, "Let no one sneer at the part that woman is taking in this revival. God is greatly honoring her, and she is confessing Him by singing, praying, and testifying. A woman's voice is often heard when the woman herself cannot be seen."[102]

How do you think this revival changed Wales?
What could a revival like this do for your
community?

Reports showed that the consumption of alcohol decreased fifty percent. Taverns closed. Crime decreased so much that there were days the judges had no cases, and many police officers became unemployed.[103]

For years the coal miners would cuss at their mules when they gave them commands. During the revival, many coal miners got saved and stopped using swear words. The mules became puzzled, and they would not follow the miner's instructions.[104]

The revival even affected local businesses. One doctor had people who owed him money. He canceled the debt because they refused to pay. After these people confessed their sins, they came to the doctor's office to pay off their debts. Others returned items they had stolen.[105]

By the end of 1904, the revival had continued for over two months. For years, people had wasted their money at the taverns and bars, not having any money for Christmas dinner or toys.

By December 25, it was agreed that it was the first Christmas for many children. Over twenty thousand homes enjoyed their first real Christmas in 1904 because parents got saved and stopped drinking. Many taverns were empty as churches filled with people giving thanks to God for what He was doing.[106]

The revival dwindled by 1906. However, the effects of the revival were long-lasting. Six years after the revival, 80 percent of the converts were members of the churches where they accepted Christ.

Roberts rested after the revival and never returned to public ministry. He devoted the rest of his life to prayer and intercession. In 1928, there were reports of him meeting a prayer group, where God used him to heal the sick. He died in 1951.[107]

Why should we always keep a burden to pray for revival?

We know the changes that revival brings in the life of a church, but what changes can revival bring in day-to-day life?

Application

Before the Welsh Revival, Wales was in a backslidden condition. Yet God made His power known, shaking and changing an entire nation.

There are two key takeaways from the Welsh Revival. First, some people experienced God do something supernatural that changed their nation twice in their lifetime.

We should never grow comfortable with a one-time

experience with God. When someone has experienced a genuine revival, it will "permanently affect their whole future lives."[108] The stories of what God did in the past impressed Roberts to contend for God to do something in his lifetime.

Second, the emphasis of the Welsh Revival was on glorifying God and confessing sin. When we prioritize spending time praising and thanking God, He will make His presence known.

Then, in His presence, conviction will come on those who need to get right. The Welsh Revival began with the cry of intercession from a man in his mid-twenties, "Lord, bend me."

God still wants to bend us and do in us what we cannot do in ourselves. Within two years, over two hundred thousand to two hundred-fifty thousand people in Wales came to Christ. We, too, need God to place a hunger for Him within us in our day. We must believe that God will do awesome things for which we did not look. He wants to come down. Lord, bend us.

Prior to experiencing God's Spirit in revival, people might seem apprehensive or fearful of giving God full control. However, when the waves of revival crash over a person, church, region, or nation, people will soon come to enjoy what they had once rejected.

How does revival forever change a person?

Is it selfish to hunger for God to pour out His
Spirit again and again?

Should we long for God to send revival at least
twice in our lifetime?

Challenge

The Welsh Revival emphasized worship, confession, and humility. Take each of these concepts and see how you can apply them to your life. Spend some time worshipping God. Then confess and sins. Then humble yourself before Him.

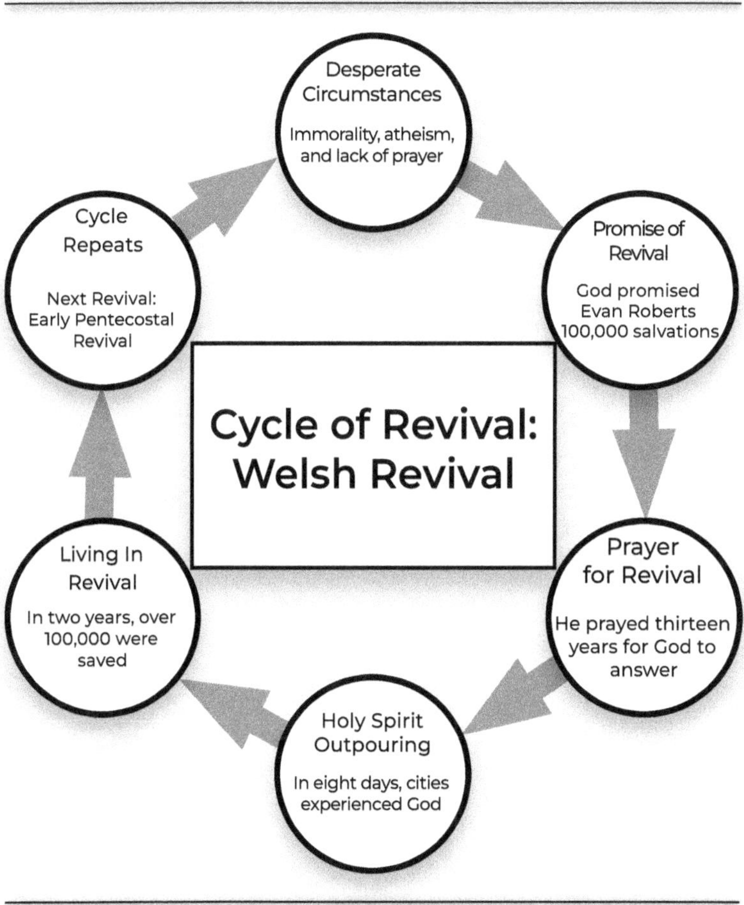

Early Pentecostal Revivals

Not long after my wife and I married, we decided to go swimming at the creek near our house. After an hour or two in the water, our great time abruptly ended.

About twenty feet from us we noticed something. At first, we thought it was stick floating with the current. After further examination, we realized it was a snake. It would peek its head up and down, peering at us having fun in the water.

We quickly exited the creek and have yet to return to swim there. Though snakes are common in creeks, rivers, or lakes, seeing one got our attention.

Just as the snake was in the water the entire time we were in the creek, Satan notices when an individual, a church, a region, or a nation pray for and experience revival.

Jesus promises in John 10, "The thief does not come except to steal, and to kill, and to destroy. I have come that they may have life, and that they may have it more abundantly" (v. 10). If the enemy can, he will do whatever it takes to steal people's attention so he can kill momentum, thereby killing revival.

The Early Church faced this reality. In Acts 10, God sent Peter to the home of a Gentile named Cornelius. The two races did not mix, but God used Peter to extend His mercy and power upon every tribe, tongue, and nation.

Initially, some in the church were concerned with Peter's ministry to the Gentiles. Peter defended what He did, showing that their experience aligned with what took place on the Day of Pentecost.

He explains in Acts 11,

And as I began to speak, the Holy Spirit fell upon them, as upon us at the beginning. Then I remembered the word of the Lord, how He said, 'John indeed baptized with water, but you shall be baptized with the Holy Spirit.' If therefore God gave them the same gift as He gave us when we believed on the Lord Jesus Christ, who was I that I could withstand God? (vv. 15-17).

While the enemy thought he could bring division within the Early Church, God gave wisdom to the leaders on how to steward the continuous yet unique outpouring of the Holy Spirit.

As the Holy Spirit empowered first-century Christians, early Pentecostal outpourings in the modern era also dramatically shifted the landscape of the global Church. In the late 1890s to the early 1900s, God poured out His Spirit, and people spoke in tongues, healed the sick, and sent missionaries worldwide with the full gospel message.

While God used various people in mighty ways, some were inflexible to the variety of ways God saved and empowered people.

What does the Holy Spirit mean to you?

Why do you think God uses a variety of ways to
reach people?

Desperate Circumstances

As with other revivals, before God poured out His Spirit, desperate circumstances occurred. Toward the end of the 1800s, God used evangelists like Charles G. Finney and Dwight L. Moody to see thousands saved. The traditional church, however, did not offer a place for them to grow in their relationship with God.[109]

The culture of the United States also changed drastically during this period. The Industrial Revolution caused cities to flourish, as many from the country sought employment in factories.

Wealth increased and decreased as the stock market fluctuated, but through all of this, church membership grew.[110] From the outside, churches appeared strong. However, through increased wealth, changing culture, and outside influence, most churches became spiritually dry.

Services became formal as they exchanged congregational singing for large choirs filled with many singers who had never made a confession of their faith. Sermons did not emphasize being born again. If someone was born to Christian parents, they too were considered a Christian.

Many pastors did not show the evidence of a genuine call to the ministry. Instead, they viewed their occupation as a profession, which meant that many Christians did not take time to tell others about Christ.[111]

The idea was that if people were ethical and helped each other, they were in good standing with God.[112]

Though most church members and clergy did not emphasize godliness and biblical living, there was a remnant of people who longed for God to do something supernatural.

Stanley Frodsham described this time in the church with a few questions. "Why do we not see miracles today as of old? The Lord Jesus went about doing good, and healing all that were oppressed of the devil. His apostles did the same. Why are we not having a like ministry today?"[113]

How do you think God feels when people want
to see revival in their lives or church?

Promise of Revival

Though many churches did not emphasize God's help and even denied biblical truth, some still longed for Him. Therefore, many became restorationists. The restoration movement wanted to restore the "original order of things as revealed in Scripture."[114]

They decided to test every aspect of the church against the practices and beliefs of the New Testament.[115] A common theme of the New Testament is God's direct participation with His people. When He got involved, signs, wonders, miracles, and healings followed.

Many shared the conviction that they were living in the "Evening Light." They quoted and declared, "It shall be one day Which is known to the Lord Neither day nor night. But at evening time it shall happen That it will be light" (Zechariah 14:7).[116]

Early Pentecostal leaders believed that God wanted to restore the church to an Apostolic Era, mirroring what God did in the New Testament.[117]

Charles Parham was among those who possessed a restorationist view.

How would you define New Testament Christianity?

What do we see in the New Testament that is not functioning equally in the church today?

Prayer for Revival

Charles Parham began studying the Bible in comparison to the modern church. In 1898, he moved his family and ministry to Topeka, Kansas.

He established the Bethel Healing Home, where he had regularly scheduled services daily. His ministry emphasized "salvation by faith; healing by faith; coming of Christ; the baptism of the Holy Ghost and Fire."[118]

In October 1900, he opened the Bethel Bible School. A group of forty students met in an old, unfinished mansion in Topeka. Many in the area called it "Stone's Folly." The school had a threefold purpose—study the Bible on various topics, pray three-hour prayer shifts, and go into the community to help people.

In December, Parham assigned the students to study the biblical evidence of the baptism in the Holy Spirit. They were to read and reread the Book of Acts. Parham met with the students on the thirty-first of December at 10:00 a.m. to see what they learned from their month-long research project.

Every student had the same conclusion; in the Book of Acts when the Holy Spirit fell, the common evidence was speaking in tongues.[119]

Do you think these students in Topeka, Kansas immediately understood how speaking in tongues would impact Christianity in the twentieth century?

Outpouring of the Holy Spirit

The students began praying New Year's Eve into New Year's Day. One of the students, Agnes Ozman, was the first to be baptized in the Holy Spirit. Here is her own account told by her:

> It was nearly eleven o'clock on this the first of January that it came into my heart to ask that hands be laid on me that I might receive the gift of the Holy Ghost. As hands

were laid upon my head, I began to speak in tongues, glorifying God, I talked in several languages. It was as though rivers of living water were proceeding from my innermost being.[120]

For the next three days, she spoke in tongues more than she did in English. During this time, while she prayed in the Spirit at a mission in Topeka, a Bohemian man told her she spoke in his language, and he understood every word she said.

Another student, Miss Lillian Thistlewaite, shared her story:

> Through the Spirit I received this message, 'Praise the Lord for the Baptism.' A great joy came into my soul and I began to say, 'I praise Thee,' and great floods of laughter came into my heart … I tried to praise the Lord in English but could not.

Thislewaite then shared how others received their Spirit baptism, and "with simultaneous movement, we began to sing together, each one singing in his new language but all in perfect harmony."[121]

How do you think these students felt when they
spoke in tongues for the first time?

Why should we praise God instead of
begging Him for His gifts?

While many were filled with the Holy Spirit on that day in Topeka and afterward, it was not the first time that people had spoken in tongues since the Day of Pentecost.

For example, there are reports of people speaking in tongues before the Civil War in 1854.[122] Again in 1873, a revival happened in New England where people spoke in tongues and the gifts of healing manifested.[123]

In the mid-1880s, the maternal grandmother of Dr. Stanley Horton, a premier Pentecostal theologian who passed away in 2014 at age 98, spoke in tongues. Clara Daisy Sanford, a speaker at Keswick conferences, stood to address a group of Baptist women near Erie, Pennsylvania.

> She felt the power of the Holy Spirit and suddenly began to speak in a language she had never learned … The women wanted to know what that 'funny foreign language' was, but she didn't know and didn't fully understand what had happened.[124]

Though people have spoken in tongues throughout history, as Stanley Burgess so aptly describes,[125] what God did in Topeka birthed the modern Pentecostal movement.[126] Many Pentecostals believe that speaking in tongues is the initial physical evidence of the baptism in the Holy Spirit.[127]

What did you think the first time you heard
someone speak in tongues?

How did you feel the first time you spoke in
tongues?

Living in Revival

The outpouring of the Spirit at Topeka was revolutionary. Supernatural living became common with those who had been baptized in the Holy Spirit. Newspaper reporters came to Topeka to record what they saw.

Articles appeared in Kansas City and St. Louis papers. People came to see what the baptism in the Holy Spirit was all about. One man went to a meeting and heard someone speak in tongues.

At the end of the service, he stood and shared, "I am healed of my infidelity; I have heard in my own tongue a Psalm I learned at my mother's knee."[128]

Though people were initially receptive, some negative reports and small crowds stalled the movement.[129] Two years after the initial outpouring in 1901, however, God sent Parham to El Dorado Springs and Joplin, Missouri.

Revival fell, and crowds of up to two thousand attended. Eight hundred people were converted to the full gospel message. In the services, people would sing in tongues and speak in tongues.

Two nuns from St. Louis visited and explained that one of the songs they heard in tongues was sung perfectly in Latin. Their Catholic church choir attempted the song but gave up because it was too difficult.[130]

God used Parham and his band of Pentecostal believers in southwest Missouri and Oklahoma, which was then still Indian territory.

What do you think it was like for those in the
early days of the Pentecostal outpouring?

Do you think everyone immediately accepted
tongues as the initial physical evidence of the
baptism in the Holy Spirit?

The Cycle Repeats

Eventually, Parham took the Pentecostal message to Houston, Texas. It was there that an African American preacher named William J. Seymour heard about Pentecost. He attended Parham's Bible school classes but had to sit away from the other students due to segregation. He eventually took the Pentecostal message to Los Angeles, where God poured out His Spirit at the Azusa Street Mission.[131]

The next chapter covers the Azusa Street revival. God did work through Charles Parham in Topeka, but He wanted to do a new thing and continue the cycle of revival into another part of the nation.

Do you think Charles Parham approved of the
Azusa Street revival?

Why would it be positive to support what God
did at Azusa?

God had used Parham mightily. His leadership had helped establish tongues as the initial physical evidence of the baptism in the Holy Spirit. However, when God wanted another wave of revival to crash in a new way in a different part of the country, Parham resisted. Specifically, he opposed God using an African American preacher to lead the Azusa Street revival. Not only did his racism hinder God's work through him, but he also became jealous and bitter at the success of what God did at Azusa.[132]

Sadly, Parham was not a part of what God did after Topeka. He spent the final two decades of his life separated from the Pentecostal movement. When he died in 1929, most second-generation Pentecostals knew very little about Parham.[133] God used him mightily at first, but when God sought to pour out His Spirit on all flesh, regardless of gender or race, Parham resisted. Satan lurked beneath the surface, ready to bring division, desiring to destroy what God had determined to accomplish.

When Parham started preaching, he believed God wanted to restore New Testament Christianity. Restorationists thought, "There is no man at the head of this movement. God Himself is speaking in the earth."[134] The Lord wanted the Pentecostal movement to be God-led, not human-led.

Can our actions and lifestyle cause us to miss
out on revival?

What happens if we do not let God have His
way?

Application

The ministry and teaching of Parham affects much of the Church today. There are Pentecostal and Charismatic congregations around the world who believe that Jesus still baptizes in the Holy Spirit and that people can still speak in tongues.

While God used Parham tremendously, when it was time for God to come down in Los Angeles, Parham was against what happened. He was unwilling to move into the next wave of revival, where God would use both genders and all races.

Why is it important that God spread His power
to all races?

When Peter showed that the Gentiles had received a biblical experience, the Early Church moved forward willing to reach anyone who will accept Jesus. What God did after Charles Parham at the Azusa Street revival was scripturally based and supernaturally empowered. Instead of moving with the wind of the Spirit, Parham resisted what God wanted to do. His life can serve as an example for us in our desire for God to send revival. We must flow where God leads us.

Does God always work the same way every
time?

What should we do when God does something
new?

If a new wave of revival is biblical and God-
honoring, how should we respond?

Challenge

Open your heart to God this week. Ask Him to do something new in you. Should you experience something in Him that has never occurred in your life, ask for wisdom and grace to receive His will. Examine your heart, and ask the Lord to show you if there is any place where you might resist Him.

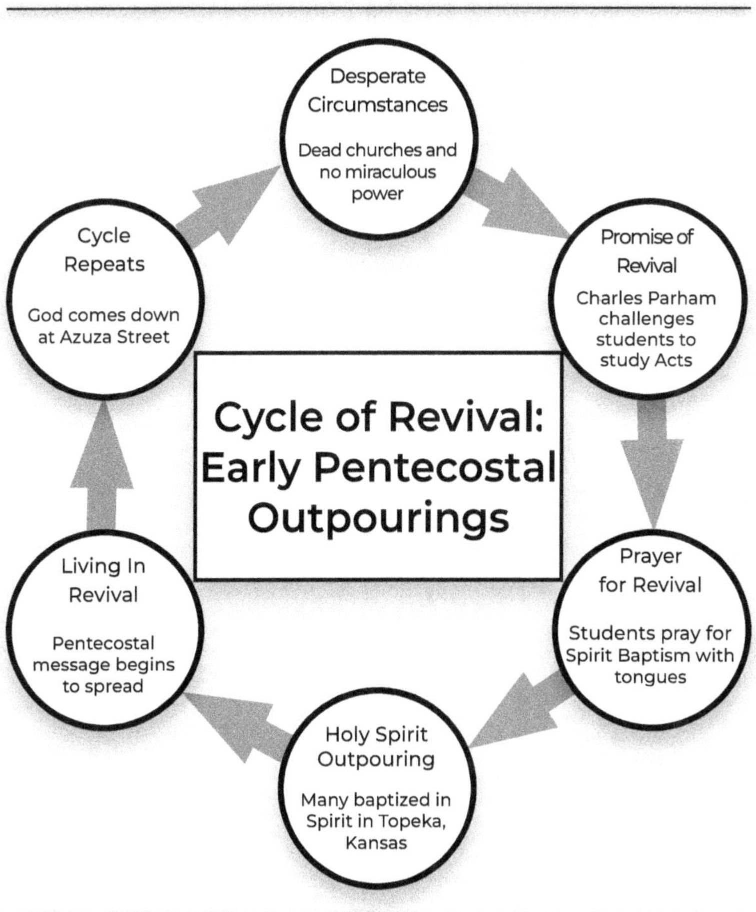

The Azusa Street Revival

Since I have lived my entire life away from the ocean, I find myself going to water parks. Designers have created these places to make it seem like the ocean. They have fake palm trees; some have sandy beaches, and most of the ones I have been to have a wave pool. These pools simulate real waves. They start off small, and eventually the waves become so large that everyone in the pool bobs up and down with the motion of the waves.

While it is fun, it is not real. The simulation does come close to what it is like when the wind blows across the ocean. It is not nearly as appealing to watch simulated waves since I have seen real waves crash onto the coast of the ocean.

Prior to His Ascension, Jesus issued a promise: "But you shall receive power when the Holy Spirit has come upon you; and you shall be witnesses to Me in Jerusalem, and in all Judea and Samaria, and to the end of the earth" (Acts 1:8). With His impending departure from earth, many of His followers questioned the future. They had experienced the real power of God while He traveled this earth. What would the future look like without Him? Jesus promised them they would have the same power He had. They would receive this power when the Holy Spirit came to them.

Ten days after He returned to heaven, the Holy Spirit fell on the crowd gathered in Jerusalem. Luke recounts, "And they were all filled with the Holy Spirit and began to speak with other tongues, as the Spirit gave them utterance" (Acts 2:4). From that point forward, the Church walked in God's supernatural power.

At the turn of the twentieth century, God worked through Charles Parham and other early Pentecostal believers to teach that speaking in tongues is the biblical evidence of the baptism in the Holy Spirit. Many people in the Midwest and the South began to accept the teaching of the Pentecostal message.

However, in Los Angeles, God stirred the hearts of people to prepare for revival. Many had grown weary of going through the motions. They longed for experiences that mirrored the Early Church.

In 1905, Pastor Joseph Smale of First Baptist Church in Los Angeles went to the Welsh Revival. For fifteen weeks, his church prayed for a similar outpouring of the Spirit. However, the church elders did not want revival and forced Pastor Smale to resign.[135]

Many from Smale's congregation joined him at his new church and renewed their prayer for God to pour out His Spirit.[136] God heard their prayer and prepared William

Seymour to help bring a revival that would change the entire world.[137]

What happens if we resist revival?

If God wants to send revival, will He find a
place that will receive what He wants?

How does God use people who
walk in His power?

Desperate Circumstances

Born to former enslaved people of African descent, God destined William J. Seymour's life for something supernatural. From a young age, he had a keen awareness of God and a hunger for His will.[138]

Seymour lived in Houston, Texas, during the time Charles Parham began to spread the Pentecostal message.

Due to segregation, he had to remain separated from the other students, but he listened to Parham's position on the baptism in the Holy Spirit.

Although he was not allowed to go to the altar to seek the baptism in the Holy Spirit, he nonetheless left the Bible school believing tongues was the initial physical evidence of the Spirit baptism.[139]

A church invited Seymour to preach in Los Angeles. When he preached, he chose his text from Acts 2:4, emphasizing tongues. The pastor of the church became offended, for she had not spoken in tongues.[140] After the morning service, he returned in the afternoon. The pastor had padlocked the door to make sure Seymour knew he was not welcome to come back to preach his doctrine of Spirit baptism.[141]

What desperate circumstancesdid Seymour face?

Why did the enemy fight him so hard?

Promise of and Prayer for Revival

Some from the mission followed Seymour. He taught them about the work of the Spirit. However, the crowds outgrew the home where they met. Richard and Ruth Asberry invited Seymour and his group to meet at their home on 214 Bonnie Brae Street. The Asberrys were Baptist and did not believe in Seymour's teaching. However, they had compassion for him being kicked out of a church.[142] For over three weeks, the group met—seeking, studying, and praying for the baptism in the Holy Spirit. Still, no one spoke in tongues, including Seymour.[143]

How do you think Seymour felt teaching
tongues as the initial evidence of Spirit baptism
but not having spoken in tongues?

Seymour corresponded with Parham, requesting help. Parham sent two workers, one who had spoken in tongues and one who had not.[144] The group committed to praying and fasting for ten days to prepare God to pour out His Spirit.[145]

One night Seymour stopped by a man's home to pray with him. When he laid his hands on him, the man began to speak in tongues. This was the first time Seymour had prayed anyone through to the Holy Spirit baptism, yet he himself had not yet spoken in tongues.

He rushed to the house on Bonnie Brae Street and shared what happened with everyone. Faith began to rise, and suddenly, Seymour and seven others fell to the floor and began to speak in tongues.[146]

The shouts of praise in the room were so vibrant and loud.[147] The Asberrys' young daughter ran out of the house terrified and excited. She told the neighbors what happened, and eventually, a crowd gathered outside the home. Those inside went to them and began to preach about the Pentecostal experience.

One of those present that night was Jennie Moore. After God filled her with the Holy Spirit, she went to the piano and began to play as she sang in tongues. Before that, she had no musical ability, but the Holy Spirit anointed her to play, and she did so the rest of her life. Eventually, she married Seymour.[148]

What do you think the neighbors thought about
what happened?

How do you think this experience change their
lives?

Outpouring of the Holy Spirit

For the next three days, the Asberrys' home became a church. The crowds grew so large that people could not get inside. They stood by open windows, attempting to hear the Pentecostal preaching.

The services on Bonnie Brae Street were not quiet. The neighbors could hear people shouting, speaking in tongues, and singing in the Spirit.[149] Eventually, many people pressed in to get in the house. The foundation collapsed, and the porch crashed into the front yard. The new group of Pentecostals quickly looked for a new building.[150]

The First African Methodist Episcopal Church had vacated their building, and it had become a livery stable and storage building. Seymour leased it for eight dollars a month. The building was in disrepair and needed much attention.[151] However, it was just the place God wanted to pour out His Spirit. People flocked to 312 Azusa Street to see what God was doing.

Local and national papers wrote about the mission. The press was not positive, but they provided free publicity. The mission took advantage of that and began writing tracts and articles telling people what God did.[152]

The Azusa Street Mission was a local congregation. They had leaders, an active membership list, and Seymour was their pastor. From 1906 to 1913, God shined on this local congregation that hungered for God's power and Spirit.[153]

God's presence was felt, and His glory was evident. Many witnessed a visible sign of God's glory—a dense cloud—hovering in the sanctuary.

Why do we need God's presence?

How will God know if we are hungry for His
presence and glory in our lives and church?

Living in Revival

The congregation at Azusa Street differed from many other
churches. They did not have a set schedule, per se.[154]

The services also lacked what most churches of the day
had. They did not use musical instruments regularly. No
one joined the choir. They often heard angels singing, while
people would spontaneously begin to sing. There was no
advertising, but everyone knew something was happening
at Azusa.[155]

Worship was a fixture of the meeting. The crowd loved
to sing their favorite song, "The Comforter Has Come."[156]

They believed that worship was their means of
encountering God. There were times when Seymour led
the entire congregation in dancing before the Lord. Other
services were more silent as people knelt and poured their
hearts out to God. In those moments, a "holy hush" would
fall over the people.[157]

When people went home, they took the presence of God
with them. One of the workers in the mission used her home
to feed the staff. They would discuss the services, and the
Lord would reveal the Holy Spirit. They explained, "The
dining room is a blessed place. The power comes down so

upon the workers that we can scarcely eat. We sing, speak in tongues, and praise God at the table."[158]

Singing in the Spirit was common. Various people worshipped and began to sing in tongues—some in perfect harmony. Seymour's wife led the singing, and she could not sing until she was baptized in the Spirit.[159]

Do praise and worship hold an important place
in your church and your life?

Why should worship be a part of our services?

Another time an evangelist came to the Azusa Street Mission to correct them. He believed they were false in their teaching and practice of speaking in tongues. He addressed the crowd, and the longer he spoke, the more convicted he became. Before he finished his speech, he fell to his knees, asking for forgiveness and praying to receive the Holy Spirit baptism. Eventually, he spoke in tongues.[160]

Many times, people outside of the mission could see a glow on the building, and it was visible a few blocks away.[161] Frank Bartleman, a reporter and Christian article writer, witnessed people get off the train a half-mile away from the mission, begin to make their way to Azusa Street, fall to the ground, and speak in tongues.[162]

Unusual miracles, signs, and wonders became common at the revival. One man, Tommy Anderson, came to the mission but always backslid and returned to alcohol. Seymour instructed him to pray whenever he passed a saloon.

He passed five saloons, kneeling, crawling, and praying past the doors, attempting to resist the lure of liquor. He crawled past the sixth, and God gave him victory. He walked past the seventh and eighth and never returned to a saloon. He became the first man to take the Pentecostal message to Ecuador, Bolivia, and Venezuela.[163]

Not everyone was in favor of what God did at Azusa Street. Many demeaning articles were written in newspapers. Cartoonists would draw their interpretation of the revival. They would "use derogatory names" to describe the actions of the Pentecostals.[164] One newspaper reporter came to give an account of the meetings of these "ignorant, fanatical, demented people." After the service began, a woman stood and urged the crowd, telling them someone needed to turn to God.

> She then broke out in tongues. It was apparent she spoke in a tongue she did not know. She gazed upon the reporter and forcefully prayed in the Spirit. After service, he asked her if she knew the language she spoke, and she promptly replied, "Not a word."

> At first, he did not believe her. Then he explained he was born in another country. He said the lady "had given an entirely correct statement of his wicked life, and that he now fully believed her utterances were exclusively from God in order to lead him to true repentance."[165]

Under the leadership of Seymour, the mission created a newspaper, *The Apostolic Faith*. Production was a group effort, but it spread the news of what God was doing around the nation and through the world. The following are selected excerpts from the newspaper.

> Meetings begin at ten o'clock in the morning and can hardly stop before ten or twelve at night, and sometimes

two or three in the morning, because so many are seeking, and some are slain under the power of God.[166]

About 150 [in September 1906] people in Los Angeles, more than on the day of Pentecost, have received the gift of the Holy Ghost and the Bible evidence, the gift of tongues, and many have been saved and sanctified, nobody knows how many. People are seeking at the altar three times a day and it is hard to close at night on account of seekers and those who are under the power of God.[167]

HEALED BY THE LORD. A sister who has had hemorrhages of the lungs for years was brought very low lately, having seven hard hemorrhages one after another. She was nearing the river [Note: an expression for nearing death] and heard her name called three times by a heavenly messenger, but she answered that she did not feel she could say she had fought a good fight and kept the faith. Then the drawing to the other shore ceased. The saints prayed for her, and she arose, and dressed perfectly healed. She went to the table and ate her dinner and afterwards played and sang several hymns. She has received the Holy Ghost and God has raised her up to preach the whole Gospel.[168]

Sister Jennie Jacobson, a Swedish sister who had been only two months in this country, was given the gift of the English language with the understanding of the words. She also received another tongue.[169]

CAME FROM ALASKA. Bro. H. M. Turney, an evangelist who was in Alaska when he heard of the outpouring of God's Spirit in California, struck out immediately for Los Angeles, and he has received the baptism with the Holy Ghost and the gift of tongues. About five minutes before he received the Holy Ghost, while kneeling at the altar, he whispered to Bro. Oyler that the devil was tempting him that the speaking in tongues was not for him. Bro. Oyler replied, "The devil is a liar from the beginning." And immediately the Holy

Ghost fell on our brother and he spoke with tongues. Since then he says the Lord waked hum up at night speaking and singing in tongues, as He has so many others.[170]

PENTECOST AMONG THE YOUNG PEOPLE. A band of Spirit filled boys went down to Anaheim, a town near Los Angeles. They testified what God had done for them and made the people hungry. The second night the altar was full. In two nights, eight were sanctified, six converted, and five received the baptism. One night at about one o'clock in the morning, the Holy Ghost spoke words in Spanish through one of the young men, and a girl who was seeking her Pentecost understood that language and joyfully interpreted it. "Keep awake, do not sleep, and I will come to thy house." This same girl within about an hour-and-a-half received the baptism with the Holy Ghost. The first to get the baptism was a little boy of ten years. He began clapping his hands and signing, "Jesus Savior, pilot me" in an unknown tongue in clear distinct words, also "Nearer my God to thee." Four in the same family inside of twenty minutes got the baptism with the Holy Ghost. It was heaven there. The work is going on and other little children are being filled with the Spirit.[171]

PENTECOST IN OTHER LANDS … We are having a wonderful time in Sweden. Hundreds have been saved and sanctified. Over a hundred baptized in the Holy Ghost. Praise God! Glory! Glory! Glory! Many have been healed by the dear Lord. Signs as on the day of Pentecost are following, talking, and singing in tongues. I cannot tell you all now that God has been doing. The work is spreading fast … Andrew G. Johnson, Address, 48 Skofde, Sweden.[172]

People receive the baptism with the Holy Ghost while about their work. One sister received hers while baking a cake.[173]

A burglar came to the altar at Azusa Mission, threw his skeleton keys under the bench (he had been plotting to rob a house). He got gloriously saved, soon he was sanctified. He was baptized down at the ocean and shouted and jumped in the water and out of the water, he was so filled with the power of God. That afternoon he was baptized with the Holy Ghost and spake in tongues. He praises God and weeps as he tells of His wonderful love and mercy.[174]

A sister finding there were some things hindering her from getting her baptism, shut herself in her room and prayed practically all day and all night. She prayed through and got all her idols out of her heart and the power fell on her "like hail." She talked in tongues for a long time, though she said when she came to the mission she did not want tongues. But God baptized her like all the rest.[175]

These are only a few excerpts from *The Apostolic Faith*, which ran in publication from 1906 to 1908.

What do these stories mean to you?

How does hearing what God did then build our
faith today?

Application

Jesus promised that believers could have power when the Holy Spirit comes upon them. God's plan for the Church is for sinners to repent and receive salvation. Once we are saved, there is a gift available, the baptism in the Holy Spirit. God sent the Spirit four different times in the book of Acts (2:1-4; 8:14-17; 10:45-48; and 19:1-7).

The common evidence of the baptism in the Holy Spirit was speaking in tongues.

Is speaking in tongues the purpose of the
baptism in the Holy Spirit?

Should we seek to speak in tongues our should
we seek Jesus as we pray for the baptism in the
Holy Spirit?

One of the concerns of some at Azusa Street was that it would become a tongues movement instead of a Jesus movement.[176] Through proper teaching, people began to understand that everything is about Jesus.

When Jesus is glorified, people will feel the conviction of sin, a desire for God's power, and healing from their sickness or problems. God uses people who long to walk in the power of the Holy Spirit. However, He uses them to point others to their need for salvation.

In 1958, Billy Graham delivered a sermon in his Sacramento, California Crusade; here is an excerpt of his message:

We have learned so much about the power of the Holy Spirit. You know, in the main denominations, we have looked a bit askance at our brethren from the Pentecostal churches because of their emphasis on the doctrine of the Holy Spirt ... I wonder if one of the secrets of Pentecostalism cannot be learned by our mainstream churches with the great emphasis on the Holy Spirit.

I am sure that my Pentecostal brethren that are here today would agree with me that there have been extremes and excesses that have embarrassed many of them at times, but I want to tell you that I believe the time has come to give the Holy Spirit His rightful place in our preaching, in our teaching, and in our churches We need to go back and study again what Paul meant when he said, "Be filled with the Spirit." We need to learn once again what it means to be baptized with the Holy Spirit …

We do not have the same enthusiasm, the same dynamics, and the same power the Early Church had. They had no Bibles, no seminaries, nor Bible Schools. No radios or telephones. No printing presses. No churches. Nothing! However, they turned the world upside down in one generation. What did they have? They had an experience with the living Christ. The had the filling of the Holy Spirit.[177]

In just over one century, God has taken the Pentecostal message from the fringes of society. Now,

as most of Christianity shrinks, Pentecostals are the fastest-growing group. A *Wheaton Theology* report says: "There were 631 million Pentecostals in 2014, comprising nearly one-fourth of all Christians. There were only 63 million Pentecostals in 1970, and the number is expected to reach 800 million by 2025."[178]

Do we need the Holy Spirit in our church?

Why are you thankful our church is a
Pentecostal church?

How has speaking in tongues been a blessing to
you?

What has Jesus done through you since you have
become aware of the Spirit's work in your life?

Challenge

God's work at Azusa Street was built on the foundation of prayer and dependence of the Holy Spirit. Make time to pray for God to do revive your life and church. If you have yet to be baptized in the Holy Spirit, ask Jesus to fill you. If you are Spirit-filled, ask God to continue to pour His Spirit out in you and pray in tongues every day.

Healing Revivals of the 1920s

Though most of my childhood vacations took place at the lake, one summer we decided to camp on the Illinois River. It felt different, especially when it came time to swim.

The campsite was five miles below the dam of Lake Tenkiller. At one point during our stay, the dam was opened, and the shallow parts of the river were deeper. It fascinated me. By that time, I enjoyed playing in deeper waters. For the rest of the week, I wanted them to open the dam and let more water flow down the river.

When I think of the flowing river, I remember Jesus's promise,

> And He said to them, "Go into all the world and preach the gospel to every creature. He who believes and is baptized will be saved; but he who does not believe will be condemned. And these signs will follow those who believe: In My name they will cast out demons; they will speak with new tongues; they will take up

serpents; and if they drink anything deadly, it will by no means hurt them; they will lay hands on the sick, and they will recover." So then, after the Lord had spoken to them, He was received up into heaven, and sat down at the right hand of God. And they went out and preached everywhere, the Lord working with them and confirming the word through the accompanying signs. Amen (Mark 16:15-20).

Through the work of the Spirit at the Azusa Street revival, the Pentecostal message spread across the world, spearheaded by the Azusa Street revival. God used early Pentecostals to rally believers to New Testament Christianity, emphasizing the unique work of the Holy Spirit in the believer.[179]

Though Pentecostals found a place in many communities, their stance on moral issues and their emphasis on speaking in tongues was a new concept to many people.[180] Even still, the winds of the Spirit began to blow, and it was as though God had opened a dam in heaven and let the healing waters begin to flow throughout the United States.

God began to use various evangelists to proclaim the healing power of Jesus. This chapter focuses on three of these evangelists: Smith Wigglesworth, Aimee Semple McPherson, and Dr. Charles Price.

Each of these ministers felt the wind of the Spirit blow over them and experienced the waves of healing in over their lives. God used their experiences to bring healing to thousands, marking their ministry within the Pentecostal movement as an era of divine healing.

Have you personally experienced God's healing
power?

Why does our personal testimony of healing
help and encourage others?

Desperate Circumstances

Born in England, Smith Wigglesworth was an uneducated
man who had a sincere desire for God. However, the process
of becoming the "Apostle of Faith" did not happen instantly.[181]

After marrying, Wigglesworth and his wife, Polly, opened
a street mission where she preached, and Wigglesworth
prayed with people after the sermon. Though he ultimately
became one of the boldest preachers of his time, it was
after twenty-five years of marriage that he preached his first
sermon. At first, he became more focused on his plumbing
business, and for two years, he stayed away from ministry
and became hardened to the Lord.[182]

Why is it easy to stray when we get sidetracked
away from God?

What distractions does the enemy provide to get
people off focus?

Promise of and Prayer for Revival

Becoming distant from God created problems for
Wigglesworth's family. He made life miserable for his wife

and the mission she led. However, his wife never ceased praying for her wayward husband. God answered her prayers and never gave up on him.

In July 1893, Wigglesworth sought God for sanctification. After ten days of intense prayer, he received a spiritual breakthrough and fully surrendered to God. His longing to live a set-apart life was key to his spiritual and character formation.[183] However, God had much more for him.

What could have happened to Smith
Wigglesworth had his wife given up on him?

How long should we pray for the salvation of
our lost loved ones?

Outpouring of the Holy Spirit

In 1907, news of the Pentecostal outpouring at Azusa Street reached England. Initially, Wigglesworth was hesitant to accept the Pentecostal teaching of Spirit baptism evidenced by tongues. In his mind, when God sanctified him, God also baptized him in the Holy Spirit.[184]

After a few days in a special service at a church in another town, God convinced Wigglesworth of his need for the baptism in the Holy Spirit. Before he went home, the pastor's wife of that church laid her hands on him, and God filled him with the Spirit.

He explained,

The power of God fell upon my body with such ecstasy of joy that I could not satisfy the joy within, with the natural tongue, then I found the Spirit speaking through me in other tongues … One time I thought I had the Holy Ghost. Now I know the Holy Ghost has got me.[185]

When he returned home, he preached an entire message for the first time. His wife, who up to that time had led all the pulpit ministry, exclaimed, "That's not my Smith, Lord; that's not my Smith!"[186] From there, God used Wigglesworth in divine and dramatic ways. An apostolic anointing came upon him, evidenced by his boldness and the signs and wonders that followed his ministry.[187]

How does the Holy Spirit help us?

Living in Revival

Six years after Jesus baptized Smith Wigglesworth in the Holy Spirit, his beloved wife passed away.[188] Then two years after her death, his youngest child, George, died. His daughter and her husband traveled with him, but she was incurably deaf in both ears.[189] His family losses and sickness led him to press into the promises of God, specifically that Jesus can still heal and deliver people.

Wigglesworth's personal experiences became a springboard for healing and revival in the lives of others. He possessed a deep, abiding faith in God. He preached, "The Word of God has not to be prayed about; the Word of God is to be received and obeyed."[190] Wigglesworth's method of prayer was peculiar and aggressive. He believed sickness was of the devil.

One man came for prayer at a healing service, dying of cancer, and Wigglesworth punched him in the stomach, causing the man to collapse. The attending doctor accused Wigglesworth of killing the man. He replied, "He's healed." In about ten minutes, the man came running down the aisle, totally healed. Wigglesworth was not impressed and continued to pray for others.[191]

God's work in Wigglesworth's life was unique to him. He displayed the cycle of revival. Through his desperation, he prayed God's promises and lived in the overflow of revival. His connection with God became a conduit of healing and blessing for others who needed salvation, healing, or supernatural power.

What can we learn from Wigglesworth's life?

Desperate Circumstances

Unlike Wigglesworth, who was rough and plain-spoken, Aimee Semple McPherson was reticent and refined. While many second-generation Pentecostals endured hardships, ridicule, and hostility, McPherson's influence reached across denominational lines.[192]

McPherson's outward success was not without personal tragedy and many desperate circumstances. She and her first husband were missionaries in China. Unfortunately, he died three months after their arrival and one month before the birth of her first daughter.[193]

Why would the enemy attack McPherson the
way he did?

Promise of and Prayer for Revival

As often happened with healing evangelists, McPherson faced a crisis in her faith and a lack of confidence in her calling. She endured many illnesses and became so sick that she hovered between life and death.[194] However, the Lord asked her a simple question: "Now—will—you—go?"[195]

She responded to God's call to return to the United States, and with her willingness to enter into a new phase of ministry, McPherson began a personal cycle of revival. Longing to preach, she took her children, was joined by her mother, and began to travel and preach the full gospel message.[196]

Why do you think McPherson answered God's
call?

Why does God want us to serve Him?

Outpouring of the Holy Spirit

As McPherson held onto God's promise to save, heal, baptize in the Spirit, and come again, crowds flocked to see her demonstrative and entertaining method of ministry. Her revival services in St. Louis in 1919 represent her experiences wherever she went.

101

Initially, the 3,000-seat auditorium appeared too large compared to the expected crowds. However, night after night, more people came to Christ and received healing.[197] Unique miracles followed as God used McPherson mightily. God healed one lady of rheumatism and cancer, enabling her to lift her hands painlessly. Braces, crutches, and canes lined the wall as testimonies of Jesus as the Physician.

As the crowds grew, more people stood outside than could come into the auditorium. God provided a new venue and the provision to rent the Coliseum in St. Louis that would seat 12,000 comfortably and 16,000 standing.[198]

The crowds watched as God healed a sixty-eight-year-old mother of her deafness. Her daughter was a beautiful singer, and the mother had never heard her voice. The crowd rejoiced as the daughter sang a hymn as the mother listened.

Complete services were made available to healing those confined to stretchers and wheelchairs. In one service, hundreds laid down their beds and cots after arriving from a steady stream of ambulances.[199]

What would it be like to see healings like this today?

What should we do when God heals some, but does not heal others?

Living in Revival

By 1923, McPherson headquartered her ministry in Los

Angeles, California. She purchased property and built Angelus Temple. At the time, it had eight large stained-glass windows, seating for over five thousand, and was the largest unsupported dome in North America.[200] Furthermore, God enabled her to build the church debt-free.[201]

Here, too, at Angelus Temple, the walls contained rows of crutches and wheelchairs from those who God healed.

Furthermore, McPherson became noted for her illustrated sermons that caught the attention of thousands who came each week to one of the five services she conducted.[202]

However, she never advertised her services, for the building could not contain the crowds that would have attended. Nevertheless, people filled the building when the doors opened, hungry for God to meet their needs.[203]

Though God used McPherson in unusual and inexplicable ways, her "public persona masked a painful loneliness."[204] Throughout her life, she endured harsh criticism as a woman in ministry.[205]

Still, God continued to use McPherson. Her life was like the Psalmist's words, "The sacrifices of God are a broken spirit, A broken and a contrite heart—These, O God, You will not despise" (Ps 51:17).

The Lord used McPherson's desperate circumstances to compel her to pray for revival. God poured out His Spirit in her life, and she lived in a state of revival, thereby leading others in the realm of the Spirit.

How did God use McPherson's personal tragedy
to help others?

Why does God use broken people?

Desperate Circumstances

Dr. Charles Price possessed a unique corner in the realm of healing evangelists. Like Wigglesworth and McPherson, Dr. Price's background became a foundation for the way God used him to reach thousands with the healing message of Christ.

Raised in a God-fearing home in England, Dr. Price enrolled in Oxford University. There, he began to question the religious nature of his upbringing, deeming it "old-fashioned and rather narrow."[206] After completing school, God led him to move to Canada, where he possessed an irresistible desire to relocate to Spokane, Washington.[207] His journey from a God-fearing home to questioning his faith proved desperately devastating.

Why is a lack of faith in God a desperate
circumstance?

What happens when we start to think we know
more than God?

Promise of and Prayer for Revival

While in Spokane, he joined a local mission and began to preach. He heard of the Pentecostal revival that took place in Los Angeles, and he began to hunger for the baptism in the Holy Spirit.[208]

As he made his way to a prayer meeting with a group of Pentecostals, a local minister dissuaded him telling him, "Price, I cannot let you go. You will wreck your future—your life. You are young and inexperienced. If you take this step, you will regret it as long as you live."[209]

Why would the enemy want to keep someone
from being baptized in the Holy Spirit?

Price listened to the ill-advised words of the pastor. He quit seeking God and ceased giving altar calls, stopped leading people to Jesus, and preached solely for the love of preaching.[210]

Price pastored a Congregational Church in Lodi, California. During that time, he began selling bonds for the War Department. His messages were intellectual, rational, and void of spiritual life.

Some in his church had an encounter with God the Holy Spirit. To disprove Pentecostalism as a fad that will soon fade, Dr. Price attended a series of revivals led by McPherson in San Jose, California.

When he entered, he recognized a familiar face, Dr. William Kenney Towner, pastor of the First Baptist Church in San Jose. He assumed Dr. Towner was there to minimize the Pentecostal movement as well.

To his surprise, Dr. Towner shouted out "GLORY" and then told Dr. Price he believed in the Pentecostal message; he confessed, "I have been baptized in the Holy Ghost."[211]

In McPherson's meetings, the blind began to see, and cripples leaped for joy. When she gave the invitation for salvation, Dr. Price put his intellectual approach aside and responded. He left the service a changed man.[212]

How does salvation change our lives?

Outpouring of the Holy Spirit

Soon after Price's conversion to the Pentecostal way, he began to seek the baptism in the Holy Spirit. He timidly hid behind the piano praying, but Dr. Towner ushered him to the middle of the room. He lifted his hand and experienced an electric feeling in his arms. He attempted to say, "Glory," but his English turned into a language he never knew.[213] His cycle of revival began with a crisis of faith. However, he heard of the promise of revival and prayed for God's Spirit. Once the Holy Spirit came upon him, he lived in a new realm—a dimension of revival.

How do you think Dr. Price felt when he fully
submitted to God?

Living in Revival

Dr. Price returned to his congregation a new man. He held "tarrying meetings" where crowds of one thousand came to seek the Holy Spirit. Soon after, he resigned from his church and began to travel with McPherson. He ministered in places where she could not.

From there, he began to hold meetings where thousands would flock to receive God's supernatural, healing power. Disabled people would walk, others spoke in tongues, and the deaf and mute would speak.[214]

So many people wanted to attend Price's packed-out meetings that in one city, some broke the windows of the building and gave money to repair the damages, just to get inside.[215]

Dr. Price influenced the Pentecostal movement in remarkable ways, especially in the Pacific Northwest. In Ashland, Oregon, so many came to experience God, Dr. Price requested Christians not to attend. They filled the auditorium, making no room for the unsaved. In that revival, an entire high school class accepted Christ, dramatically changing their school's culture. He moved to Seattle, Washington, where God saved and healed hundreds.[216]

Dr. Price was unassuming in his approach. Observers recognized "the unfeigned humility with which God has so graciously clothed him, and with it the wonderful ability and power of the Holy Spirit enabling him to minister in such a remarkable way."[217]

Dr. Price conducted services at Faith Tabernacle in Oklahoma City, OK, in 1928.[218] One of the attendees of the services was Elmer T. Watkins, the son of a circuit-riding Methodist minister.

When Watkins was fifteen years old, he had developed a rare blood disorder. The doctors gave a grim prognosis of a shortened life. Since his father traveled, his mother took him to Faith Tabernacle.

They walked from their home to downtown Oklahoma City, taking breaks for the boy to catch his breath. At the service, Dr. Price prayed a simple prayer and laid his hands on him. Instantly, God healed him.

At the same time, his mother burst out speaking in tongues and could not speak in English for four to five days. To his father's surprise, his Methodist wife became Pentecostal, and his son was cured of an incurable disease.

For some time, the elder Watkins struggled with what happened to his family. He read and reread the Book of Acts, eventually asking God to show him whether the Pentecostal message was true or false. Instantly, he too was baptized in the Holy Spirit.[219]

Elmer Watkins became a leader in the Assemblies of God in Oklahoma.[220] His daughter and son-in-law, Betty and J. R. Tucker, evangelized throughout the country and pastored in California and Oklahoma.

J. R. Tucker was my pastor and one of my mentors. Throughout the formative years of my spiritual formation, I listened as he shared how their family was dramatically transformed because Dr. Price lived in a supernatural dimension.

Though I did not know Dr. Price or Elmer Watkins, I can trace my spiritual life and my hunger for God to pour out His Spirit back to the healing revivals of the 1920s.

What connection do you see between the
baptism in the Holy Spirit and God's ability to
heal people?

Is there any sickness too hard for God to heal?

Application

God used Wigglesworth, McPherson, and Dr. Price at a critical juncture in the up-and-coming Pentecostal movement. However, the Lord took the three of them to heaven in the mid-forties.

At the time of their death, their concern of the "dying interest" of evangelism surfaced. Furthermore, it did not appear that there were "new recruits to fill the vacancies" of the departed faith healers.[221] As they neared death, they looked for a day when greater miracles would come for future generations.

In 1936, Wigglesworth prophesied about future revivals, where even mainline denominations would experience the revival and the gifts of the Holy Spirit.[222] God's revelation of future revival came to pass into the twentieth century with the Charismatic Renewal. Wigglesworth is widely associated with faith and healing. Additionally, before his death, Dr. Price prophesied of a coming revival that would "break even the most calloused hearts."[223]

McPherson's work did not die with her either. She founded the Foursquare Church. Its organization as of 2023 has over 8.8 million members in over 67,500 churches across more than 150 nations.[224]

Jesus promised that power would come to His followers. He instructed them to go and make disciples. When His followers make the decision to tell others about Jesus, He will confirm His word with signs following.

Why does God send signs, wonders, and miracles?

What do healings and miracles do to those who are not right with God?

Who can God use to pray for those who are sick?

Challenge

God still heals today. Take time to see if there is any area of your life—spiritual, physical, emotional, or relational—that needs healing. Then ask Him to heal that specific area in your life. Ask Him to make you a conduit of healing, being able to pray for the sick and see them recover.

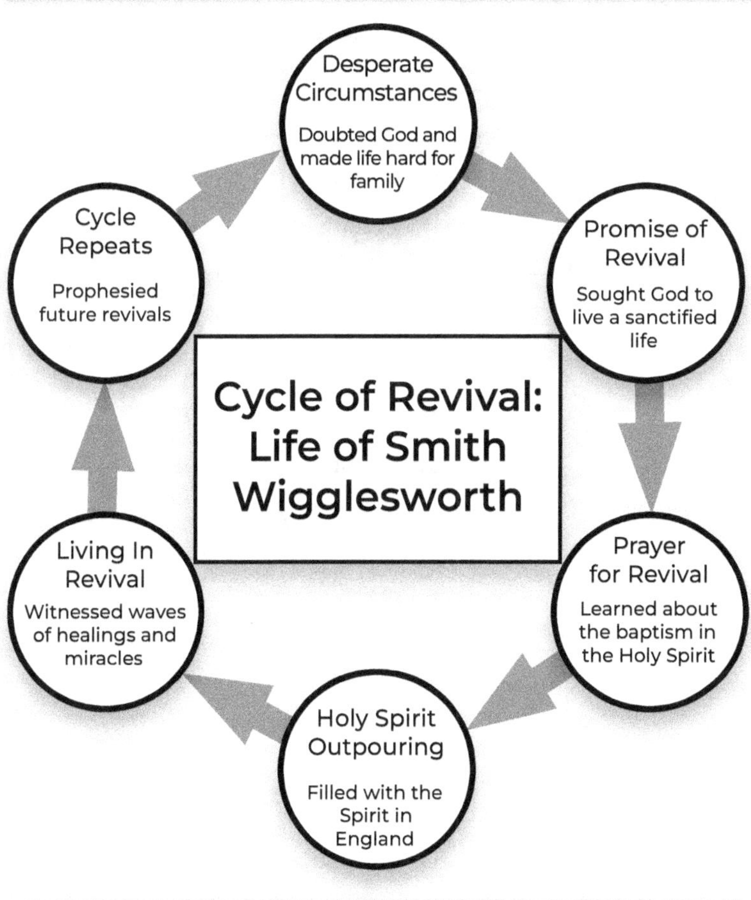

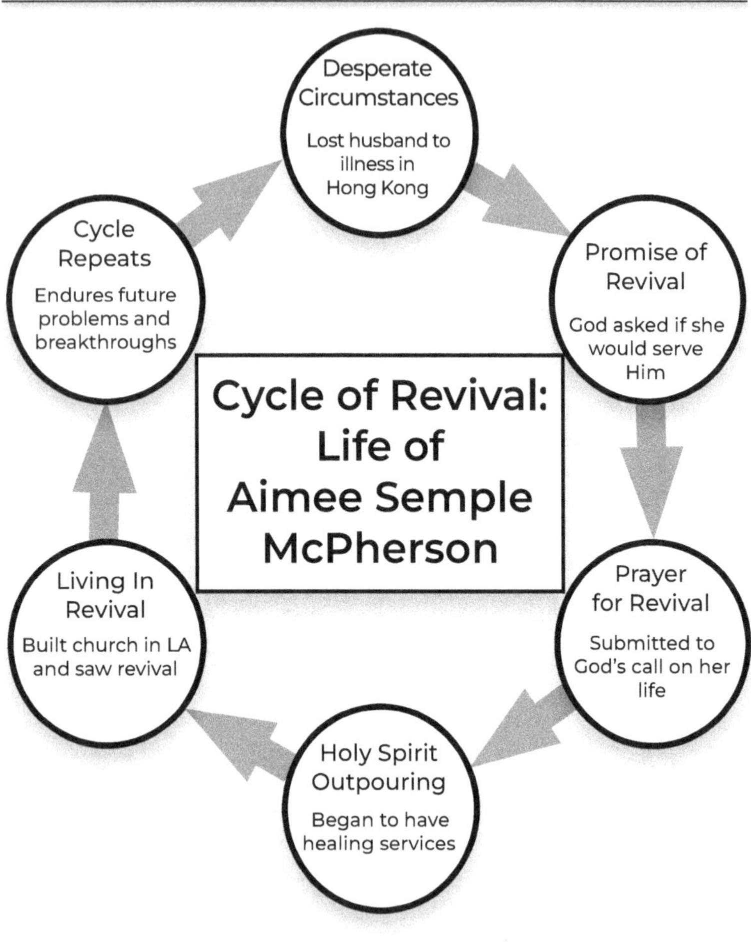

Desperate Circumstances
Lost husband to illness in Hong Kong
Cycle Repeats
Endures future problems and breakthroughs
Promise of Revival
God asked if she would serve Him
Cycle of Revival: Life of Aimee Semple McPherson
Living In Revival
Built church in LA and saw revival
Prayer for Revival
Submitted to God's call on her life
Holy Spirit Outpouring
Began to have healing services

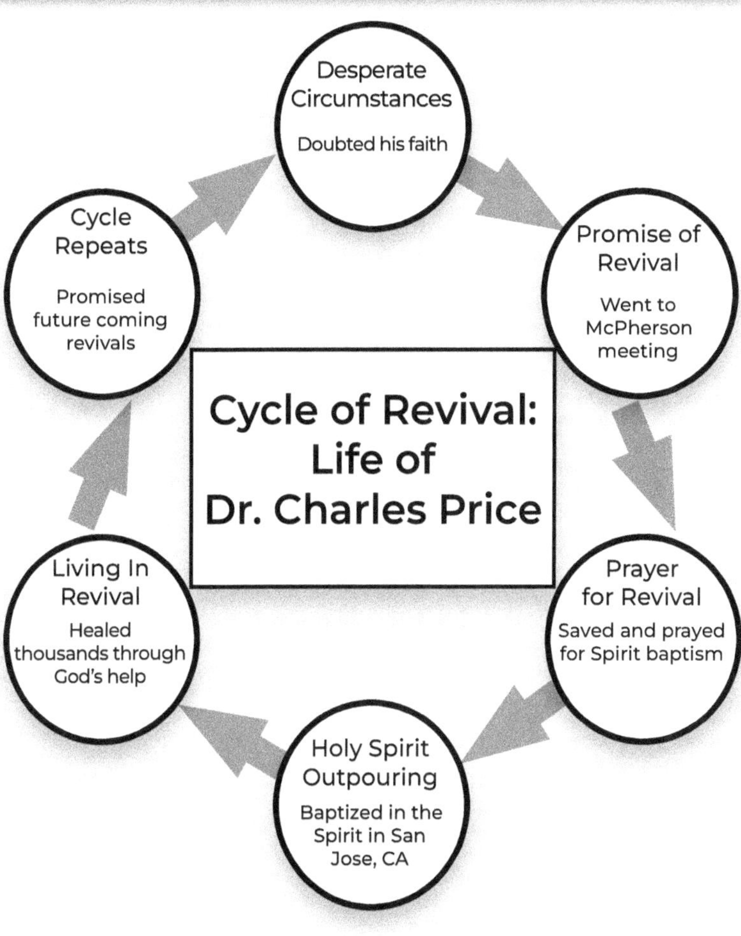
Desperate Circumstances
Doubted his faith
Cycle Repeats
Promised future coming revivals
Promise of Revival
Went to McPherson meeting
Cycle of Revival: Life of Dr. Charles Price
Living In Revival
Healed thousands through God's help
Prayer for Revival
Saved and prayed for Spirit baptism
Holy Spirit Outpouring
Baptized in the Spirit in San Jose, CA

Hebrides Revival

I have witnessed God's artistry in many places—from the Atlantic to the Pacific Oceans, to the Rocky and Appalachian Mountains. In my opinion, He chose to create His masterpiece nestled in Ozarks.

I live in a rural part of Missouri. A favorite pastime of many in my community is to take a boat on the river. Because I cannot operate the boat, I get the privilege of riding and watching the scenery. I feel abundantly fortunate to live in a remote part of the country. Riding on the river reminds me that God creates some of His best work in places most people do not know exist.

Sometimes revival comes to entire nations. Other times it changes regions. Then there are revivals that come to obscure places that many people do not know exists.

God told King Asa, "For the eyes of the Lord run to and fro throughout the whole earth, to show Himself strong on behalf of those whose heart is loyal to Him" (2 Chronicles

16:9). When God sends revival, He does not focus on what is marketable or accessible. Instead, He looks for people who will allow the wind of the Spirit to blow over their prayers and intercession.

North of Scotland rests a collection of islands called the Outer Hebrides. From 1949-1952, God sent a revival to two of the islands there—Lewis and Harris. Combined, these two islands make up 891 square miles, smaller than the state of Rhode Island. They had a population of about 25,000, with 21,000 of them living in country villages, far from society.[225]

Though the inhabitants of the Hebrides were out of sight, they were not out of God's mind. On the islands, God used the intercession of a few to shake the towns and villages for three years with His convicting presence.

Should living in a remote town or attending a
small church limit our prayers?

Why is God interested in small communities?

Desperate Circumstances

Though the Hebrides are isolated from much of the world, they were not exempt from Satan's attacks. Like other places, before revival came, the church had dwindled, and people showed indifference toward God. Before the revival, young people displayed little interest in God. They spent their Sundays in bed or drinking alcohol.[226] Every town was witnessing the same trend. Not a single young person attended worship. They would read or walk, but they were not concerned about coming to God's house.[227]

What will happen to a church if younger people
and families do not get involved?

Why is it tempting to schedule other activities
on Sunday instead of going to church?

Promise of and Prayer for Revival

The lack of interest in God's house stirred the hearts of some intercessors from the town of Barvas. God gave a burden to two sisters, Peggy and Christine Smith. Peggy was eighty-four and blind, and Christine was eighty-two and bent over with arthritis. They knew about the low crowds at their church and the lack of participation from young people. However, "rather than complain, they chose to pray."[228]

They declared God's promise, "For I will pour out water on him who is thirsty, and floods on the dry ground. I will pour out my Spirit on your descendants, and My blessing on your offspring" (Isaiah 44:3).[229]

The sisters trusted God to keep His covenant with His people. Therefore, they committed to pray on Tuesday and Friday every week. They would get on their knees at 10:00 p.m. and seek God until 3:00 to 4:00 a.m., trusting Him to reach their community.

Peggy, who was blind, had a vision of her church being so full of so many young people and families that there was not an empty seat. She called her pastor, who believed God spoke to her.[230]

One of the sisters encouraged the pastor to do something about the vision. They suggested he call the elders and deacons of his church to meet in a barn every Tuesday and Friday to pray while the sisters would pray in their home.[231]

After several months of prayer, one of the younger deacons stood to read: "Who shall ascend into the hill of the Lord? Or who shall stand in His holy place? He that hath clean hands and a pure heart—he shall receive the blessings of the Lord" (Psalms 24:3-5).

Then he asked the other men, "We have been praying for months for revival, waiting before God, but I would like to ask you now: are our hands clean? Is the heart pure?"[232]

When he asked those questions, the Lord came down, and he fell into a trance, lying on the floor of the barn. Conviction gripped everyone present. They began to ask God to clean their hands and purify their hearts.[233]

The power of God started to flow from that barn into the church. One of the sisters encouraged the pastor to invite a minister to come. She did not know who, but in her vision, she saw a man she did not know standing in the pulpit.[234]

Why do you think the sisters and the elders of
the church prayed the way they did?

Why does God require clean hands and a pure
heart (holiness) to experience His blessings and
revival?

Outpouring of the Holy Spirit

The local pastor invited a Scottish minister named Duncan Campbell. Initially, he declined the invitation because he had other services scheduled. However, they were canceled, and he went to Lewis, one of the Hebrides Islands. He planned to stay for ten days.

He arrived, and the pastor asked if he was willing to meet with the church at 9:00 that evening. He agreed, and 300 people gathered to listen to him preach. At 10:45 p.m., he dismissed the congregation when the young deacon, who prayed in the barn, cried out, "God, you can't fail us. God, you can't fail us. You promised to pour water on the thirsty and floods upon the dry ground. God, you can't fail us!" He fell to his knees to pray and entered into a trance.[235]

Suddenly, the back door of the church opened, and someone shouted, "Something wonderful has happened. Oh, we were praying that God would pour water on the thirsty and floods upon the dry ground and listen, He's done it! He's done it!"

Outside stood 600 people who felt drawn by God's Spirit to get to the church. Many of them were young people who were partying and felt a conviction they did not understand. They noticed the lights on at the church and began running there.

The rest of the crowd were entire families who awoke from their sleep and did not know why. They got dressed and went to the church. Everyone went back inside. It was midnight, and people were kneeling, laying prostrate, or sitting—crying out for mercy. God fulfilled the vision He had given the blind sister, Peggy.[236]

The service lasted until 4:00 a.m. As Pastor Campbell left the church, someone told him he needed to get to the police station. Next door to the police station was the home of the two sisters who had prayed for revival. It is as though God's magnetic power was drawing those who were far from God.

Surrounding the station, people repented of their sins. One of the young men was drunk, but God saved him, and he became a pastor. The scene outside the station looked like what had happened at the church.[237]

Do you think anyone expected revival to come
the way it did?

Who decides how and when revival comes?

Living in Revival

For the next three years, revival spread across the island. Services lasted until 3:00 a.m.[238] A messenger came to one congregation to tell them that the church fifteen miles away was also crowded with people seeking God.[239]

One of the small villages, Arnol, had not experienced the revival yet. A church elder invited Pastor Campbell to join them in a prayer meeting. It was winter, and the church did not have heat, so they met in a farmhouse.

A group of thirty prayer warriors gathered, and a man stood to pray. He called on God for about half an hour and then paused. He looked to heaven and concluded his prayer:

"You promised to pour water on the thirsty and floods on the dry ground and God, You're not doing it!"

He prayed a little longer and then paused. After a moment of silence, he cried out, "God, Your honor is at stake, I now take it upon myself to challenge you to fulfill Your covenant engagement!"

How do you think God responded to his bold
prayer?

It was 2:00 a.m., and as soon as he prayed, the house shook, a pitcher fell from the counter and broke. At the same time, God's Spirit came to the village. People woke up from their homes and gathered in the streets under conviction.

That night, the local bar closed down and did not open again. Fifteen years after that night, fourteen of the town drunks were still in church and attended prayer meeting three times a week, praying for God to send revival again.[240]

An awareness of God swept through village after village. Sinners could not resist the conviction of the Spirit. One man heard about salvation and resisted the message. He went to the bar to drink his way out of what he felt. However, there were other men in the bar who discussed feeling convicted and feared they would be eternally lost. He then went to the dance hall and thought he could dance his way out of what he felt. On the dance floor a young lady came to him and asked, "Oh, where would eternity find us, if God should strike us dead tonight?" He felt so convicted that he stopped, surrendered himself to Christ, and repented of his sins.[241]

Pastor Campbell went to one church and felt resistance to what God wanted to do. A fifteen-year-old boy traveled with him. As Pastor Campbell struggled to preach, he stopped and asked the boy, Donald, to lead in prayer. As Donald closed his prayer, he lifted his eyes and cried, "Oh God, I seem to be gazing through the open door. I see the Lamb in the midst of the Throne, with the keys of death and of hell at His girdle." He began to sob, lifting his eyes toward heaven, and cried: "O God, there is power there, let it loose!"

Immediately it was as though a hurricane swept through the building. Heaven opened over the congregation, and the church looked like a battlefield. People fell and sobbed, asking God to save them from their sin.[242]

In 1968, Pastor Campbell told of a time Peggy felt he was to go to a community. There were seven men there who needed salvation. God told Peggy that these seven men would become pillars in the church there.

Pastor Campbell told her, "I have no leadings to go to that village." She replied, "Mr. Campbell, if you were living as near to God as you ought to be, He would reveal His secrets to you also."

When he arrived at the village, he saw seven men. They listened to his message and were all saved within a matter of days. Later, he found out that these men were all Communists and wanted nothing to do with God. Once they found Jesus, however, they became pillars in the church.[243]

These are just a few stories of what God did in and through the prayers of his people in the Hebrides. For three years, churches filled as people sought God. Communities fell under conviction and experienced radical conversion. Some villages hardly had one person unaffected by the revival.[244]

What would a revival like this do for your community?

Why is it encouraging that God came to villages and churches that only had a few hundred people or less?

Application

One of the seven men who prayed in the barn for five months before revival came was interviewed in 2000. In between the interviewer's questions, he would weep, sing hymns, and quote Scriptures. Fifty years later, the revival still touched his heart.[245]

Why do you think God sent revival to the Hebrides?

By the end of the revival, more people attended prayer meetings than had attended church services before the revival came. In nearly every home there was a family altar.[246]

What is a family altar, and why
do we need them?

Prayer is the reason God did what He did in the Hebrides. When the two sisters in their eighties could no longer attend church, they prayed. When the leadership of the congregation heard about Peggy's vision, they prayed. Everything they did was centered on prayer.

They believed God's Word was His covenant. Therefore, they trusted that He would keep His covenant. God did not overlook the Hebrides. Even though they were a small collection of islands with only a few people living there, God responded to their prayers.

Does the size of your community limit God's
ability to send revival?

In what ways does your community need
revival?

Challenge

God desires to visit people, churches, and communities that remain hungry for Him. Ask yourself, Does my life indicate that I long for God? Am I spiritually dry? If so, ask Him to send His rain on you, saturating you with His presence. Think of those in your life and church, and pray for God to do something unique and supernatural. Trust that He will draw all generations in your church closer to Him.

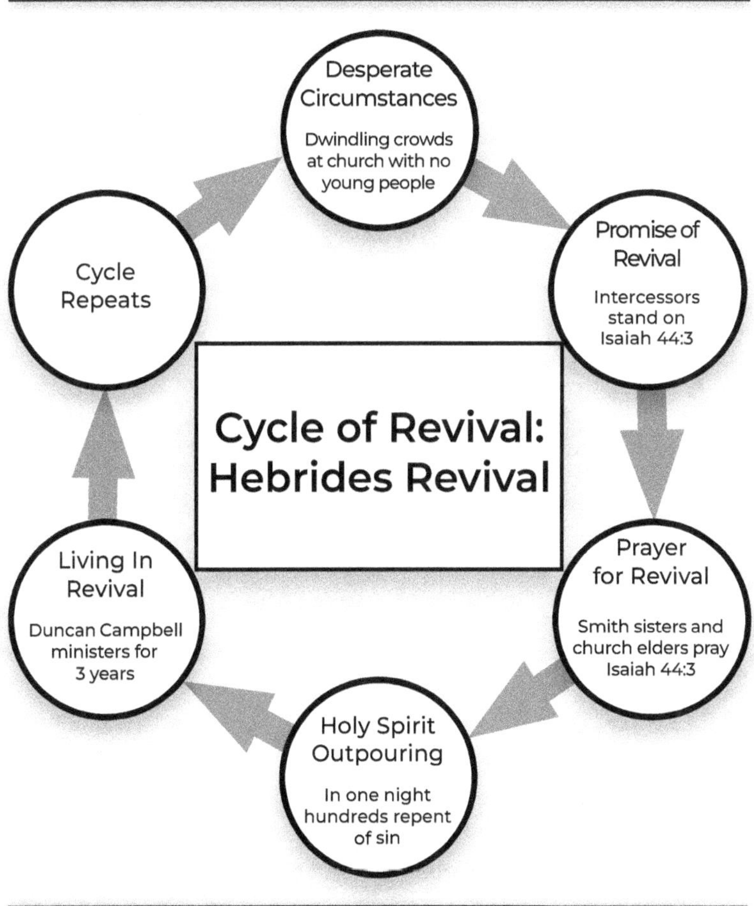

Argentine Revivals

As much as my wife and I loved the drive on Highway One in California, we couldn't help but notice the danger that surrounded the car. If we were not careful to stay on the road, we could hit jagged rocks on one side or risk falling into the ocean on the other side.

The sights were beautiful, but we had to be on our guard. I kept my hands on the steering wheel and took the curves slowly, and my wife helped me watch for traffic. The ocean waves, though appealing to the eye, did not come without their potential hazards.

The same can be said of revival. People might pray for years for revival to come, but once it arrives, it is imperative that every participant stay alert in spiritual warfare and intercession.

The Prophet Daniel had a divine experience. He had a vision from God. He knew God had promised something to him, but he didn't know what it was. Therefore, he prayed and fasted for three weeks.

Finally, an angel came with the answer, but first, he explained what took so long:

> Then he said to me, "Do not fear, Daniel, for from the first day that you set your heart to understand, and to humble yourself before your God, your words were heard; and I have come because of your words. But the prince of the kingdom of Persia withstood me twenty-one days; and behold, Michael, one of the chief princes, came to help me, for I had been left alone there with the kings of Persia. Now I have come to make you understand what will happen to your people in the latter days, for the vision refers to many days yet to come" (Daniel 10:12-14).

The moment Daniel prayed, God heard, but the enemy fought against the angel who brought the answer. Daniel's spiritual warfare was necessary in seeing God bring the much-needed answer.

What would have happened if Daniel had stopped praying before his answer came?

The threat of Satan's assault on revival should not detour people from seeking God and enjoying the waves of revival. What God did in Argentina proves this point.

In 1850, Missionary Allen Gardiner, a ship's captain, and seven other missionaries left Britain to reach southern Argentina for Christ. With limited resources, supplies, and money, they struggled tremendously.

By September 1851, each of the men died of starvation. In his journal, Gardner's final entry reads, "I trust [that] poor Fuega and South America will not be abandoned.

The missionary seed has been sown there, and the Gospel message ought to follow."[247]

God heard that prayer. Nearly a century later, revival came to the South American country. For decades, Argentina has experienced the cycle of revival more than once.

What is spiritual warfare?

Why is spiritual warfare necessary in revival?

Desperate Circumstances

One of the first waves of revival to come to Argentina occurred in the early 1950s. Before God sent His Spirit, Argentina was at a low point. Evangelicals and Pentecostals were in the minority of religious affiliation. The total number of Evangelicals was 574 in the entire nation, and Pentecostals made up a fraction of them.[248] Catholicism ruled the country. Many people knew about God but did not have a personal relationship with Him.

Why is it a problem for a nation when people
know about God but do not have a personal
relationship with Him?

Promise of and Prayer for Revival

Knowing the desperate circumstances of the nation, God led a small group of missionaries to pray. In 1948, a dozen students enrolled in the River Plate Bible Institute. In 1951, they began to pray earnestly for God to pour out His Spirit.

One night, a Polish immigrant student began to pray outside in a field. Suddenly, the presence of God consumed him, and a bright light surrounded him. He turned and saw "a shining, glorious being" behind him, and he knew that God had sent an angel.[249]

He rushed back to the dorms of the school. He beat on the locked doors until a student let him inside. He assumed that the angel would stay outside, but it followed him into the building. For the next three months, the angelic visitor continued to return to the school.

The students prayed for more than two years before God sent revival. Sometimes they would intercede so intensely that a pool of tears would form at their feet. During that time, many mocked them because it seemed that Argentina was too resistant to God.[250]

How would you feel if God sent an angel when you prayed?

As the students prayed for revival, God spoke to an evangelist named Tommy Hicks from Tallahassee, Florida. He had a vision of a map of South America and knew God wanted him to go there and preach. He did mission work in Spanish-speaking countries but did not know anything about Argentina or their president.[251]

While God spoke to Pastor Hicks, some in Argentina began to pray for an evangelistic campaign in Buenos Aires, the capital. They invited a well-known evangelist from the United States, but he was unavailable. Then they asked Pastor Hicks to come.

Pastor Hicks was very particular in what he felt God wanted to do. He requested a soccer stadium that seated 25,000 as well as the use of public radio and advertising. The committee that invited him believed that what he wanted was impossible.[252]

Even though it seemed that his expectations would not work, Pastor Hicks flew to Argentina. On the flight, he heard the Lord speak one word to him: "Perón." He asked the flight attendant if she knew a Perón. She explained, "That is our president."

Pastor Hicks knew God wanted him to persuade President Perón to allow an evangelistic campaign in one of their soccer stadiums. The local church leaders discouraged him from going to the presidential palace, but Pastor Hicks insisted on seeing the president.[253]

When he arrived, a guard asked what he wanted, and Hicks explained that he desired to hold a healing and salvation crusade. In the conversation, Pastor Hicks prayed for the guard. When they finished praying, God healed the guard instantly.

He told him to return the next day to meet President Perón. The president had stayed away from the public because of a skin condition he had developed. However, as Pastor Hicks explained that God could heal, the president asked, "Do you believe that Jesus Christ heals today the same as He did while He was on earth?"

Pastor Hicks prayed for him, and "before the eyes of all present, the skin of President Perón became as clean, as soft, and as clear as a baby; he was made instantly whole."[254] The president gave Pastor Hicks everything he needed. He could use any stadium he wanted. He also had free access to the state-owned radio and newspaper.

How do you think the president felt
when he was healed?

How would healing like this affect your
community/nation?

Outpouring of the Holy Spirit

When the campaign started, the stadium that seated 25,000 filled quickly. People would arrive several hours early to fill the bleachers. Ushers worked twelve-hour shifts to accommodate the crowds that came to hear from God.

R. Edward Miller, a missionary in Argentina, explained, "the evangelist preached a simple sermon about Jesus, the Savior and Healer, (for he was not a great orator)." People responded and cried out for Jesus to heal them.

Pastor Hicks prayed the prayer of faith, and instantly people began to do what they could not do when they entered the stadium. People laid down their crutches, stood up from their wheelchairs, and even blind people began to see for the first time.

God poured out His Spirit so strongly that people did not want the campaign to end. People filled the stadium night after night. When Pastor Hicks announced that the campaign would come to a close, the crowds stood and shouted for fifteen minutes, "Let it go on! Let Hicks remain!"[255]

Can you share about a time God healed you?

Why does God still heal people today?

Living in Revival

The miracles, signs, and wonders under the ministry of Pastor Hicks continued for fifty-two days.

The crowds grew so large that they moved to another stadium that seated 180,000. People would camp out overnight to make sure they got a seat the next day. The stadium would fill to capacity, and no one else could find a seat. However, people would touch the walls from the outside and get healed. Ambulances brought people on stretchers to the services, and they would get healed and walk out of the meeting without assistance.[256]

Local bookstores ran out of Bibles. Surrounding nations began to send Bibles, and people would even pay expensive amounts to get a Bible. The crowds, once quiet and reserved in church, became emotional as they sang, shouted, and worshipped God.

Many were curious about what God did. However, whenever someone in a business or factory questioned the campaign, someone would stand and share their testimony of God's healing.

God healed hundreds of thousands. The paralyzed could walk, the blind could see, and the sick were made well. The rich, the poor, the old, the young, and those from all walks of life came to experience what God did.[257]

Over two million people heard the gospel during the fifty-two days, and over 200,000 came to Christ.[258]

What would have happened if people had not
prayed for God to send revival?

How do you think those who prayed for revival
felt when God poured out His Spirit?

Cycle Repeats/Desperate Circumstances

By the 1980s, God was ready to send another wave of revival to Argentina. The nation was at a low point morally, politically, and spiritually.[259]

Many felt that the government and the military had failed them. President Perón lost power in the 1950s, but he returned to office as president in 1973. He turned to Jose Lopez Rega, who was nicknamed "the warlock." He led the government for a few years and even built a public monument to witchcraft.[260] Much of the population got involved with voodoo and witchcraft.

Do you think the government's involvement in
demonic activity affected the nation?

Why was it necessary for the church in
Argentina to pray at this point in their history?

Promise of and Prayer for Revival

One pastor, Alberto Scataglini, called on the young people of his church to pray. Of the nearly sixty students, only six came to the prayer meeting. Nevertheless, the Lord promised them that He would do something special in 1984. By the end of their year of prayer, the youth group grew to 200, and the church grew to 500.[261]

As God stirred Pastor Scataglini's heart, the Lord prepared an unknown evangelist named Carlos Annacondia to bring revival to Argentina. Before his conversion, he was an agnostic business owner. However, God saved him.

The day his family came to Christ, all of them were baptized in the Holy Spirit. After his wife was filled with the Spirit, Annacondia cried out to God, "Baptize me in the Holy Spirit, or I'm going to die." He began to speak in tongues for ten hours. In the days that followed, he would think he was talking to someone in Spanish and was actually speaking in tongues.[262]

God prepared him for the wave of revival He wanted to send. Annacondia asked Scataglina if he could hold his first evangelistic campaign there in La Plata. Scataglini had heard about Annacondia but was unsure about him because he did not have much theological training. However, the Lord spoke to him, "Participate in the campaign, and do everything he says. This is my servant."[263]

How does the baptism in the Holy Spirit change our lives?

Why does God honor our obedience?

Outpouring of the Spirit

Even though Annacondia's vision was unconventional, the local churches participated in his crusade. He set up a separate tent from where the services took place for those who needed deliverance from demonic possession.

He kept the tent separate to protect the person's dignity and give the necessary space and time to pray the demon-possessed person through to freedom.[264] Witches and warlocks covered the area where he preached. However, they came to the services and were delivered.

In one of the early services, some of the neighbors called to complain about the noisy campaign. The chief of police sent two police officers, but they did not return. He sent four more officers, and they did not return. The chief went to the meeting and discovered that his officers were getting delivered from the enemy in the "intensive care tent."[265]

The first campaign in La Plata lasted eight months. During that time, fifty thousand people came to Christ, including many witch doctors in the area. Revival came to Argentina again.

Why should we never let the enemy
intimidate us?

Living in Revival

Revival spread through Argentina. Many of the Christian leaders describe their recent church history "before Annacondia" and "after Annacondia."[266] Annacondia did not get in a hurry when he went to a new city, and he would stay until he felt God had made a spiritual impact on the town. The longer he stayed, the more heaven would open.[267]

Another key to living in revival was their emphasis on prayer. There was space under the platform for 500 people to intercede through the meetings. One thousand would sign up, and they would take shifts to pray for what God would do that night.[268]

Why is prayer necessary in revival?

Though God used Annacondia, he was one of many who helped in the revival. Local churches exploded with growth. Young evangelists began to preach and heal the sick. One evangelist prayed for a woman with cancer. She was pale and slumped in a wheelchair in the hospital. He prayed for her, and she was instantly and permanently healed.[269]

Another young evangelist had a unique miracle. A pastor asked him to pray for a t-shirt. He later found out that the t-shirt belonged to a paralyzed man who was bound to his bed. When the shirt was placed on him, he felt fire begin to burn him. He got up from the bed and began to run around the house, fully and totally healed.[270]

Application

God has sent revival to Argentina many times. Generation after generation has experienced waves of God's Spirit. One of the keys to God's activity in Argentina is prayer. Pastor Alberto Scataglini explains, "Prayer becomes the way of life." It is "the breathing mechanism of the believer."[271]

Another Argentinian pastor believes, "If there is one dominant element that has emerged in the theology and methodology of evangelism in Argentina, I would say it is spiritual warfare."[272] Before God sent revival to Argentina, a remnant of people would pray. God responded to their intercession and sent His Spirit. Though they prayed, the enemy resisted them. That resistance is called spiritual warfare.

If the enemy is fighting against people who pray, it means they are on the right track. Therefore, they must stay steadfast in their prayer life until God sends the answer.

The Argentine Revivals are a story of people who prayed during deep spiritual darkness. God listened to their cry and sent revival to the land.

Do we live in a time of spiritual darkness?

How have you experienced spiritual warfare?

Why would the enemy fight against people who
pray for revival?

Challenge

Take time to pray about the status of your nation, state, or community. Does it need revival? If so, pray for God to give you a burden to seek Him for His Spirit's outpouring. Make yourself available to God and let Him use you in any way He sees fit. Ask God for a hunger to be filled with the Holy Spirit.

Desperate Circumstances
Very few Pentecostals/ Evangelicals
Cycle Repeats
Occultism and witchcraft increase
Promise of Revival
Angelic visitor to Bible Institute in Buenos Aires
Cycle of Revival: Argentine Revival in 1950s
Living In Revival
Over 200,000 saved in two months
Prayer for Revival
Students pray for and prophesy coming revival
Holy Spirit Outpouring
Tommy Hicks comes to Argentina

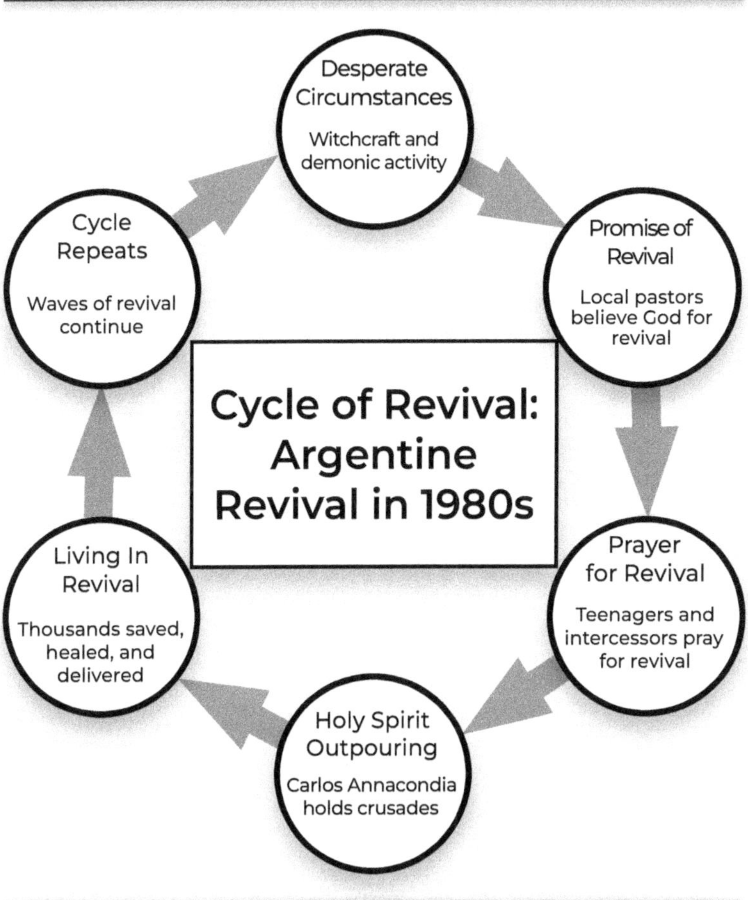

Desperate Circumstances
Witchcraft and demonic activity
Promise of Revival
Local pastors believe God for revival
Cycle Repeats
Waves of revival continue
Cycle of Revival: Argentine Revival in 1980s
Prayer for Revival
Teenagers and intercessors pray for revival
Living In Revival
Thousands saved, healed, and delivered
Holy Spirit Outpouring
Carlos Annacondia holds crusades

Conclusion

Is there anything too hard for God? Can times ever get too bad for God? Would God really want to help pull humanity from the brink of the abyss? The Psalmist also made a similar query, "Will You not revive us again, That Your people may rejoice in You?" (Ps 85:6).

The nine revivals we covered in this book do not even begin to scratch the surface of the waves of the Spirit that have rolled in on people, congregations, communities, and nations since the inception of the Church. Instead, my aim has been to whet the appetite of the reader to hold onto God's promise of revival and to pray for God to pour out His Spirit.

Each time I read and reread what God did for people in the past, I remember the words of the Apostle Peter, "In truth I perceive that God shows no partiality" (Acts 10:34). God does not play favorites. The principles discussed in each revival hold true now. Whenever people seek His will and sincerely hunger for Him, all they must do is wait and get ready for Him to pour out His Spirit.

Are we ready?

Are we preparing now for what God wants to do next?

After submitting my manuscript to the editor, my family and I went to Fort Walton Beach, Florida for our vacation.

It was the first time I spent that much time on the water. The first day, I went to catch some waves. As I stood about waste deep patiently waiting for the water to crash over me, I noticed something. The waves kept coming in on my left and right and seemed to miss me. Hurriedly, I would rush to them, but when I got there, they were gone. Finally, I determined to stay in one spot and not move. It worked. Wave after wave kept rolling onto the beach.

In the midst of the fun, I felt the Lord speak to my spirit. Often in revival, we will look at other places where God is pouring out His Spirit, and wonder why is that not happening in my life? Instead of rushing elsewhere, if we will stay put, hold onto God's promises, pray, and seek Him, when the time is right, the Lord will send His Spirit from heaven in a new way.

Everything we see in our world points to the hope that we are on the cusp of another wave of revival. Will you join in with what God wants to do? Will you become a participant of this next great outpouring of the Holy Spirit? If so, now is the hour to pray and trust God, for He really does want to revive us again.

About the Author

Daniel R. Tidmore resides in Vulcan, Missouri. In addition to being a husband and father, he and his wife pastor a loving congregation. He is an ordained minister and student at the Assemblies of God Theological Seminary in the Doctor of Ministry program. Regularly he speaks in other churches, emphasizing the work and need for the Holy Spirit.

Sources Cited

"200 Years of the Census in … WALES." Count Me in Census 2001. Accessed April 18, 2022. https://web.archive.org/web/20090319202324if_/http://www.statistics.gov.uk/census2001/bicentenary/pdfs/wales.pdf.

"1984 Argentina Revival." Beautiful Feet. Accessed April 25, 2022, https://romans1015.com/1984-argentine-revival/.

Aker, Benny. "Initial Evidence, A Biblical Perspective." In *Dictionary of Pentecostal and Charismatic Movements*, edited by Stanley M. Burgess, Gary B. McGee, and Patrick H. Alexander, 455-459. Grand Rapids, MI: Zondervan Publishing House, 1988.

"American Enlightenment Thought." Internet Encyclopedia of Philosophy." Accessed August 23, 2021. https://iep.utm.edu/amer-enl/.

"The Awesome Argentina Revival." Accessed September 22, 2021. https://thestandard.org.uk/the-blog/item/the-awesome-argentina-revival.

Blumhofer, Edith L. *The Assemblies of God: A Chapter in the Story of American Pentecostalism Volume 1- to 1941*. Springfield, MO: Gospel Publishing House, 1989.

———. *Pentecost in My Soul: Explorations in the Meaning of Pentecostal Experience in the Early Assemblies of God*. Springfield, MO: Gospel Publishing House, 1989.

————. *Restoring the Faith: The Assemblies of God, Pentecostalism, and American Culture*. Urbana and Chicago, IL: University of Chicago Press, 1993.

Brumback, Carl. *Suddenly ... From Heaven: A History of the Assemblies of God*. Springfield, MO: Gospel Publishing House, 1961.

Burke, Bob. *Like a Prairie Fire: A History of the Assemblies of God in Oklahoma*. Oklahoma City, OK: The Oklahoma District Council of the Assemblies of God, 1994.

Campbell, Duncan. *The Lewis Awakening: Revival in the Hebrides*. N.p.: Independently Published, 2017.

C. S. Lewis Institute. "Revival Born in a Prayer Meeting." Fall 2004. Knowing & Doing: A Teaching Quarterly for Discipleship of Heart and Mind. Accessed August 25, 2021. https://www.cslewisinstitute.org/webfm_send/577.

Dorries, David W. "The Making of Smith Wigglesworth Part One: The Making of the Man." *Assemblies of God Heritage* (1992): 4-8, 32.

Duewel, Wesley. *Revival Fire*. Grand Rapids, MI: Zondervan Publishing House, 1995.

Enloe, Tim. "Dr. Charles S. Price: His Life, Ministry, and Influence." *Assemblies of God Heritage* (2008): 4-13.

"Evans, Annie Florence ('Florrie') (1884-1967), Revivalist and Missionary," Y Bywgraffiadur Cymreig Dictionary of Welsh Biography, accessed May 26, 2022, https://biography.wales/article/s12-EVAN-FLO-1884.

"Events | Charles Finney's Rochester Revival | Timeline." The Association of Religion Data Archives." Accessed August 25, 2021. https://www.thearda.com/timeline/events/event_246.asp.

Finney, Charles. *How to Experience Revival*. New Ed. New Kensington, PA: Whitaker House, 2017.

Frodsham, Stanley Howard. *With Signs Following*. Springfield, MO: Gospel Publishing House, 1946.

"Get Ready for 'The Coming Revival—Dr. Charles S. Price's Prediction from 75 Years Ago! | Flower Pentecostal Heritage Center." Accessed September 27, 2021. https://ifphc.wordpress.com/2014/07/15/get-ready-for-the-coming-revival-dr-charles-s-prices-prediction-from-75-years-ago/.

Girdler, Joseph S., and Carolyn Tennant. *Keys to the Apostolic and Prophetic: Embracing the Authentic Avoiding the Bizarre*. Crestwood, KY: Meadow Streams Publishing, 2019.

Goff, Jr., J. R. "Parham, Charles Fox (1873-1929)." In *Dictionary of Pentecostal and Charismatic Movements*, edited by Stanley M. Burgess, Gary B. McGee, and Patrick H. Alexander, 660-61. Grand Rapids, MI: Zondervan Publishing House, 1988.

Goodrich, Arthur, Evan Roberts, G. Campbell Morgan, W. T. Stead, Evan Hopkins, and Others. *The Story of the Welsh Revival as Told by Eyewitnesses Together with a Sketch of Evan Roberts and His Message to the World*. Lawton, OK: Trumpet Press, 1905.

Grams, Rocky. *In Awe of Argentina*. Lake Mary, FL: Creation House, 2006.

"History." *The Foursquare Church*. Last modified November 10, 2017. Accessed September 27, 2021. https://www.foursquare.org/about/history/.

Johnson, James E. "Charles Finney." *Christian History | Learn the History of Christianity & the Church*. Accessed August 25, 2021. https://www.christianitytoday.com/history/people/evangelistsandapologists/charles-finney.html.

Lemley, Kristi. *Ablaze: Prepare Your Heart for Revival*. Tustin, CA: Trilogy Christian Publishers, 2020.

McGee, Gary B. *People of the Spirit*. Springfield, MO: Gospel Publishing House, 2004.

McIntosh, Ron. *The Quest for Revival*. Tulsa, OK: Harrison House, 1994.

McNemar, Richard. *The Kentucky Revival*. Chicago: Great Plains Press, 2011.

Menzies, William W. *Anointed to Serve: The Story of the Assemblies of God*. Springfield, MO: Gospel Publishing House, 1971.

Miller, R. Edward. *Secrets of the Argentine Revival*. Peniel Outreach Ministries, Inc., 1999.

Murphy, Owen. *When God Stepped Down from Heaven*. N.p.: Center Mark Press, Amazon Digital Services, 2012.

N4CM. "One-Fourth of Christians 'Speak in Tongues.'" Church and State. May 2, 2018. Accessed September 30, 2021. http://churchandstate.org.uk/2018/05/one-fourth-of-christians-speak-in-tongues/.

Newby, Bill, James E. Griggs, and Steve D. Eustler. *Perpetuating Pentecost: A History of the First 75 Years of the Southern Missouri District of the Assemblies of God.* Springfield, MO: Southern Missouri District Council of the Assemblies of God, 1989.

Norris, Daniel K. *Trail of Fire.* Lake Mary, FL: Charisma House, 2016.

Olena, Lois E. *Stanley M. Horton: Shaper of Pentecostal Theology.* Springfield, MO: Gospel Publishing House, 2009.

Owens, Robert. "The Azusa Street Revival: The Pentecostal Movement Begins in America." In *The Century of the Holy Spirit: 100 Years of Pentecostal and Charismatic Renewal,* edited by Vinson Synan, 39-68. Nashville, TN: Thomas Nelson, 2001.

Pettit, Steve. "Fulton Street Revival: Stories of Revival." *BJUToday,* last modified February 15, 2018. Accessed April 18, 2022. https://today.bju.edu/president/fulton-street-revival/.

Pratney, Winkie. *Revival: Principles to Change the World.* Pensacola, FL: Christian Life Books, 1984.

Price, Charles S. *The Story of My Life.* Yuma, CO: Jawbone Digital, 2017.

"Revival at Cane Ridge | Christian History Magazine." *Christian History Institute.* Accessed August 25, 2021. https://christianhistoryinstitute.org/magazine/article/revival-at-cane-ridge.

"Revival in the Hebrides (1949)." Adapted from writings by Duncan Campbell and others. (Compiled by Jim Meletiou, transcribed from a tape by Duncan Campbell made in 1968). Accessed September 24, 2021. https://notjustnotes.webs.com/Hebrides.pdf.

Robeck, Jr., Cecil M. *The Azusa Street Mission and Revival.* Nashville, TN: Thomas Nelson, Inc., 2006.

"Second Great Awakening | Description, History, and Key Figures." *Encyclopedia Britannica.* Accessed August 23, 2021. https://www.britannica.com/topic/Second-Great-Awakening.

Semple McPherson, Aimee. *This Is That.* Los Angeles, CA: Foursquare Publications, 1923.

Stewart, Marjorie. "A Story of Pentecost in the Pacific Northwest." *Assemblies of God Heritage* (Spring 1987): 3-4, 7-9 and (Summer 1987): 15-19.

Tennant, Carolyn. "'Unit 4—The Spirit-Filled Leader' (Class Notes for Core 1 Course at Assemblies of God Theological Seminary, Springfield, MO)." October 17, 2019.

———. "'Unit 6—The Second Great Awakening' (Class Notes for Revival Course at Assemblies of God Theological Seminary, Springfield, MO)." August 23, 2021.

"Tommy Hicks: El Primer Avivamiento En Argentina Que Alcanzó a Juan Domingo Perón." Enfoque Evangélico. Accessed September 22, 2021. https://enfoqueevangelico.com.ar/tommy-hicks-el-primer-avivamiento-en-argentina-que-alcanzo-a-juan-domingo-peron/.

Towns, Elmer, and Douglas Porter. *The Ten Greatest Revivals Ever.* Ann Arbor, MI: Servant Publications, 2000.

Tribken, Robert. "The Fulton Street Prayer Meetings and the Revival of 1857/58: The Workplace Connection." March

26, 2019. Center for Faith and Enterprise. Accessed April 18, 2022. https://faithandenterprise.org/wp-content/uploads/2019/04/Fulton-Street-032919.pdf.

US Department of Commerce. National Oceanic and Atmospheric Administration. "Why Does the Ocean Have Waves?" Accessed February 25, 2022. https://oceanservice.noaa.gov/facts/wavesinocean.html.

Welchel, Tommy, and Michelle Griffith. *True Stories of the Miracles of Azusa Street and Beyond.* Shippensburg, PA: Destiny Image Publishers, Inc., 2013.

"What Causes Ocean Waves?: Ocean Exploration Facts: NOAA Office of Ocean Exploration and Research." Accessed February 25, 2022. https://oceanexplorer.noaa.gov/facts/waves.html.

Wigglesworth, Smith. *Smith Wigglesworth on the Holy Spirit.* New Kensington, PA: Whitaker House, 1999.

The Apostolic Faith

"Bible Pentecost." *The Apostolic Faith*, November 1906, 2.

"Fires Are Being Kindled," *The Apostolic Faith*, May 1908., 1.

"Pentecost Has Come." *The Apostolic Faith*, September 1906, 1.

"Pentecost With Signs Following." *The Apostolic Faith*, December 1906, 1.

"Pentecost Both Sides of the Ocean." *The Apostolic Faith*, March 1907, 1.

"The Pentecostal Baptism Restored." *The Apostolic Faith*, October 1906, 4.

Picture Gallery

John Wesley (1703-1791), portrait, head and shoulders;
from a steel engraving; circa 1800s.

John Wesley (1703-1791) preaching on his father's grave; lithograph by Currier & Ives; circa 1800s.

George Whitefield (1714-1770) preaching;
from an engraving; 1857.

Charles Grandison Finney, portrait, head and shoulders; engraving; circa 1870s. Halftone.

Postcard of Evan Roberts, the Welsh revivalist, sitting at a desk; circa early 1900s.

Portrait, head and shoulders. Charles F. Parham, who at one time pastored a Methodist church in Kansas, founded a Bible school in Topeka where the Pentecostal movement began in 1901.

Frontal view of Stone's Folly, also known as Stone's Mansion, in Topeka, Kansas; circa 1901.

Agnes Ozman LaBerge standing outside her home; 1937.

Agnes N. Ozman was the first to speak in tongues at Charles F. Parham's Bethel Bible School in Topeka, Kansas, in January 1901.

Exterior view of Charles F. Parham's Bible school in Houston, Texas, located at 503 Rusk Avenue; 1906. Signs on the house say: 'Apostolic Faith Movement' and 'Headquarters.'

Richard and Ruth Asberry's home at 214 N. Bonnie Brae Street in downtown Los Angeles; circa 1906.
The first week of meetings of the Azusa Street Revival were held in this home.

Exterior view of the Azusa Street Mission; 1928. View from street. Name on side of building says 'Apostolic Faith Gospel Mission.'
Cars passing in front; seated in the car in the foreground is Louis F. Turnbull, pastor of Bethel Temple, Los Angeles.

Smith Wigglesworth at age 87
sitting in a chair; 1946.

Smith Wigglesworth laying hands on a sick child at
Angelus Temple in Los Angeles, California; 1927.
His daughter, Alice Wigglesworth Salter
is standing on the right.

AN AIMEE SEMPLE McPHERSON PUBLICATION
The BRIDAL CALL
Foursquare
BIRTHDAY NUMBER.
Not by might nor by power, but by my Spirit saith the Lord.
iFPHC.org
AIMEE

Left: Aimee Semple McPherson featured on the front cover of Bridal Call Foursquare magazine, August 1927.

Below: A crowd of people in front of Angelus Temple, Los Angeles, California, standing in line to view Aimee Semple McPherson's body, on October 8, 1944. The funeral would be the next day.

Portrait, head and shoulders. Photograph is signed: '
With Best Wishes, Preaching His Gospel, Charles S. Price.'

Charles S. Price on stage and audience seated for
Charles S. Price campaign at Massey Hall,
Toronto, Ontario.

Rev. Duncan Campbell, leader of the Hebrides Revival, portrait, with his wife; circa 1950s.

Rev. Duncan Campbell, leader of the Hebrides Revival (center), standing with prayer warrior sisters Peggy and Christine Smith; circa 1950s.

Evangelist Tommy Hicks standing behind an Argentinian flag with local pastors and others in the background at the Tommy Hicks Buenos Aires Argentina crusade; 1954.

Endnotes

Chapter 1: Waves of Revival

1   National Oceanic and Atmospheric Administration US Department of Commerce, "Why Does the Ocean Have Waves?" accessed February 25, 2022, https://oceanservice.noaa.gov/facts/wavesinocean.html.

2   All Scripture references, unless otherwise noted, are from the New Kings James Version.

3   Kristi Lemley, *Ablaze: Prepare Your Heart for Revival* (Tustin, CA: Trilogy Christian Publishers, 2020), 29.

4   Winkie Pratney, *Revival: Principles to Change the World* (Pensacola, FL: Christian Life Books, 1984), 18.

5   Ibid., 19.

6   Charles Finney, *How to Experience Revival*, new ed. (New Kensington, PA: Whitaker House, 2017), 7.

7   Carolyn Tennant, "'Unit 4—The Spirit-Filled Leader' (Class Notes for Core 1 Course at Assemblies of God Theological Seminary, Springfield, MO)," October 17, 2019.

8   "What Causes Ocean Waves? : Ocean Exploration Facts: NOAA Office of Ocean Exploration and Research," accessed February 25, 2022, https://oceanexplorer.noaa.gov/facts/waves.html.

Chapter 2: The First Great Awakening

9   Brendan Kennedy, "Repentance," ed. John D. Barry et al., *The Lexham Bible Dictionary* (Bellingham, WA: Lexham Press, 2016), Logos Bible Software.

10   Wesley Duewel, *Revival Fire* (Grand Rapids, MI: Zondervan Publishing House, 1995), 50.

11   Ibid., 51.

12   Pratney, *Revival*, 64.

13   Wesley Duewel, *Revival Fire* (Grand Rapids, MI: Zondervan Publishing House, 1995, 73-74.

14   Elmer Towns and Douglas Porter, *The Ten Greatest Revivals Ever* (Ann Arbor, MI: Servant Publications, 2000), 49.

15   Pratney, *Revival*, 65.

16   Towns and Porter, *The Ten Greatest Revivals Ever*, 62.

17   Duewel, *Revival Fire*, 51.

18   Pratney, *Revival*, 67.

19   Duewel, *Revival Fire*, 77.

20   Pratney, *Revival*, 82.

21   Ibid., 84.

22   Duewel, *Revival Fire*, 58-62.

23   Ibid., 70.

24   Daniel K. Norris, *Trail of Fire* (Lake Mary, FL: Charisma House, 2016), 15.

25   Pratney, *Revival*, 93.

26   Norris, *Trail of Fire*, 21.

27   Pratney, *Revival*, 92.

28   Towns and Porter, *The Ten Greatest Revivals Ever*, 58.

29   Duewel, *Revival Fire*, 77.

30   Pratney, *Revival*, 98-99.

Chapter 3: The Second Great Awakening

31   Towns and Porter, *The Ten Greatest Revivals Ever*, 69.

32   "American Enlightenment Thought, " Internet Encyclopedia of Philosophy, accessed August 23, 2021, https://iep.utm.edu/amer-enl/.

33   Pratney, *Revival*, 103.

34   Towns and Porter, *The Ten Greatest Revivals Ever*, 84.

35   J. Edwin Orr, "Prayer and Revival," accessed October 3, 2021, https://jedwinorr.com/resources/articles/prayandrevival.pdf, 1.

36   "Second Great Awakening | Description, History, and Key Figures," *Encyclopedia Britannica*, accessed August 23, 2021, https://www.britannica.com/topic/Second-Great-Awakening.

37   Towns and Porter, *The Ten Greatest Revivals Ever*, 75.

38   Pratney, *Revival*, 105.

39   Daniel K. Norris, *Trail of Fire* (Lake Mary, FL: Charisma House, 2016), 37.

40   "Revival at Cane Ridge | Christian History Magazine," *Christian History Institute*, accessed August 25, 2021, https://christianhistoryinstitute.org/magazine/article/revival-at-cane-ridge.

41   Towns and Porter, *The Ten Greatest Revivals Ever*, 77.

42   Norris, *Trail of Fire*, 40.

43   Ibid., 41.

44   "Revival at Cane Ridge | Christian History Magazine."

45   Towns and Porter, *The Ten Greatest Revivals Ever*, 79.

46   Ibid., 83-84.

47   Duewel, *Revival Fire*, 93-94.

48   Pratney, *Revival*, 116.

49   Duewel, *Revival Fire*, 101-103.

50   Ibid., 107.

51   James E. Johnson, "Charles Finney," *Christian History | Learn the History of Christianity & the Church*, accessed August 25, 2021, https://www.christianitytoday.com/history/people/ evangelistsandapologists/charles-finney.html.

52   Duewel, *Revival Fire*, 109.

53   "Events | Charles Finney's Rochester Revival | Timeline, " The Association of Religion Data Archives, accessed August 25, 2021, https://www.thearda.com/timeline/events/event_246.asp.

54   Towns and Porter, *The Ten Greatest Revivals Ever*, 102.

55   Ibid., 85.

56   Ibid., 86.

57   Richard McNemar, *The Kentucky Revival* (Chicago: Great Plains Press, 2011), 8.

58   Charles Finney, *How to Experience Revival*, new ed. (New Kensington, PA: Whitaker House, 2017), 7.

Chapter 4: The 1857-1859 Prayer Revival

59   C. S. Lewis Institute, "Revival Born in a Prayer Meeting," Fall 2004, Knowing & Doing: A Teaching Quarterly for Discipleship of Heart and Mind, accessed August 25, 2021, https://www. cslewisinstitute.org/webfm_send/577.

60   Pratney, *Revival*, 129-130.

61   Robert Tribken, "The Fulton Street Prayer Meetings and the Revival of 1857/58: The Workplace Connection," March 26, 2019, Center for Faith and Enterprise, accessed April 18, 2022, https://faithandenterprise.org/wp-content/uploads/2019/04/Fulton-Street-032919.pdf, 3.

62   Steve Pettit, "Fulton Street Revival: Stories of Revival," *BJUToday*, last modified February 15, 2018, accessed April 18, 2022, https://today.bju.edu/president/fulton-street-revival/.

63 Lewis Institute, "Revival."
64 Duewel, *Revival Fire*, 128.
65 Tribken, "Fulton Street," 3-4.
66 Lewis Institute, "Revival."
67 Duewel, *Revival Fire*, 128.
68 Lewis Institute, "Revival."
69 Ibid.
70 Ibid.
71 Tribken, "Fulton Street," 2.
72 Pettit, "Fulton Street Revival."
73 Towns and Porter, *The Ten Greatest Revivals Ever*, 125.
74 Lewis Institute, "Revival."
75 Ibid., 4.
76 Duewel, *Revival Fire*, 130-133.
77 Towns and Porter, *The Ten Greatest Revivals Ever*, 128.
78 Duewel, *Revival Fire*, 141.
79 Ibid., 165-166.

Chapter 5: The Welsh Revival

80 Arthur Goodrich et al., *The Story of the Welsh Revival as Told by Eyewitnesses Together with a Sketch of Evan Roberts and His Message to the World* (Lawton, OK: Trumpet Press, 1905), 14.
81 Ibid., 9-11.
82 Ibid., 7.
83 Ibid., 14.
84 Duewel, *Revival Fire*, 185.
85 Towns and Porter, *The Ten Greatest Revivals Ever*, 18.
86 Duewel, *Revival Fire*, 186.
87 Towns and Porter, *The Ten Greatest Revivals Ever*, 19.
88 Goodrich et al.,*The Story of the Welsh Revival*, 16-17.
89 Ibid., 115.
90 Duewel, *Revival Fire*, 179-180.
91 Ibid., 186.
92 "200 Years of the Census in … WALES," Count Me in Census 2001, accessed April 18, 2022, https://web.archive.org/web/20090319202324if_/http://www.statistics.gov.uk/census2001/bicentenary/pdfs/wales.pdf.
93 Duewel, *Revival Fire*, 187.
94 Norris, *Trail of Fire*, 110-11.
95 Ibid., 189-190.

96 Norris, *Trail of Fire*, 111.
97 Duewel, *Revival Fire*, 191.
98 Ibid., 193.
99 Goodrich et al., *The Story of the Welsh Revival*, 39-42.
100 Ibid., 81.
101 "Evans, Annie Florence ('Florrie') (1884-1967), Revivalist and Missionary," Y Bywgraffiadur Cymreig Dictionary of Welsh Biography, accessed May 26, 2022, https://biography.wales/article/s12-EVAN-FLO-1884.
102 S.B. Shaw, *The Great Revival in Wales* (Pensacola, FL: Christian Life Books, 2014), 70-71.
103 Norris, *Trail of Fire*, 115.
104 Goodrich et al., *The Story of the Welsh Revival*, 117-118.
105 Ibid., 148.
106 Ibid., 151.
107 Pratney, *Revival*, 200.
108 Ibid., 12.

Chapter 6: Early Pentecostal Revivals

109 Bob Burke, *Like a Prairie Fire: A History of the Assemblies of God in Oklahoma* (Oklahoma City, OK: The Oklahoma District Council of the Assemblies of God, 1994), 15.
110 William W. Menzies, *Anointed to Serve: The Story of the Assemblies of God* (Springfield, MO: Gospel Publishing House, 1971), 17.
111 Carl Brumback, *Suddenly... From Heaven: A History of the Assemblies of God* (Springfield, MO: Gospel Publishing House, 1961), 3-6.
112 Menzies, *Anointed to Serve*, 22.
113 Stanley Howard Frodsham, *With Signs Following* (Springfield, MO: Gospel Publishing House, 1946), 7.
114 Edith L. Blumhofer, *Restoring the Faith: The Assemblies of God, Pentecostalism, and American Culture* (Urbana and Chicago, IL: University of Chicago Press, 1993), 12.
115 Ibid., 13.
116 Ibid., 11.
117 Ibid., 18.
118 Edith L. Blumhofer, *The Assemblies of God: A Chapter in the Story of American Pentecostalism Volume 1- to 1941* (Springfield, MO: Gospel Publishing House, 1989), 71-73.

119 Menzies, *Anointed to Serve*, 36-37.
120 Frodsham, *With Signs Following*, 20.
121 Ibid., 21.
122 Frodsham, *With Signs Following*, 9.
123 Ibid.
124 Lois E. Olena, *Stanley M. Horton: Shaper of Pentecostal Theology* (Springfield, MO: Gospel Publishing House, 2009), 24-25.
125 Stanley M. Burgess, ed., *Christian Peoples of the Spirit: A Documentary History of Pentecostal Spirituality from the Early Church to the Present* (NYU Press, 2011).
126 Menzies, *Anointed to Serve*, 37.
127 Benny Aker, "Initial Evidence, A Biblical Perspective," in *Dictionary of Pentecostal and Charismatic Movements*, ed. Stanley M. Burgess, Gary B. McGee, and Patrick H. Alexander (Grand Rapids, MI: Zondervan Publishing House, 1988), 455.
128 Frodsham, *With Signs Following*, 22.
129 J. R. Goff, Jr., "Parham, Charles Fox (1873-1929)," in *Dictionary of Pentecostal and Charismatic Movements*, ed. Stanley M. Burgess, Gary B. McGee, and Patrick H. Alexander (Grand Rapids, MI: Zondervan Publishing House, 1988), 660-61.
130 Bill Newby, James E. Griggs, and Steve D. Eustler, *Perpetuating Pentecost: A History of the First 75 Years of the Southern Missouri District of the Assemblies of God* (Springfield, MO: Southern Missouri District Council of the Assemblies of God, 1989), 5-6.
131 Blumhofer, *Restoring the Faith*, 55.
132 Blumhofer, *The Assemblies of God Vol. 1*, 109.
133 Goff, "Parham," 661.
134 Blumhofer, *Restoring the Faith*, 91-92.

Chapter 7: The Azusa Street Revival

135 Brumback, *Suddenly*, 34-35.
136 Blumhofer, *Restoring the Faith*, 102.
137 Brumback, *Suddenly*, 35.
138 Robert Owens, "The Azusa Street Revival: The Pentecostal Movement Begins in America," in *The Century of the Holy Spirit: 100 Years of Pentecostal and Charismatic Renewal*, ed. Vinson Synan (Nashville, TN: Thomas Nelson, 2001), 46.
139 Cecil M. Robeck, Jr., *The Azusa Street Mission and Revival* (Nashville, TN: Thomas Nelson, Inc., 2006), 46-47.
140 Brumback, *Suddenly*, 35-36.

141 Menzies, *Anointed to Serve*, 50.

142 Owens, "Azusa Street Revival," 47.

143 Robeck, *Azusa Street Mission and Revival*, 65-66.

144 Owens, "Azusa Street Revival," 48.

145 Robeck, *Azusa Street Mission and Revival*, 65-66.

146 Owens, "Azusa Street Revival," 49.

147 Menzies, *Anointed to Serve*, 50.

148 Owens, "Azusa Street Revival," 48-49.

149 Robeck, *Azusa Street Mission and Revival*, 69.

150 Owens, "Azusa Street Revival," 50.

151 Robeck, *Azusa Street Mission and Revival*, 70-72.

152 Owens, "Azusa Street Revival,"53.

153 Robeck, *Azusa Street Mission and Revival*, 88.

154 Blumhofer, *Assemblies of God Vol. 1*, 103.

155 Menzies, *Anointed to Serve*, 51.

156 Brumback, *Suddenly*, 43.

157 Robeck, *Azusa Street Mission and Revival*, 133.

158 Ibid., 142.

159 Ibid., 149.

160 Ibid., 92-93.

161 Owens, "Azusa Street Revival," 53.

162 Tommy Welchel and Michelle Griffith, *True Stories of the Miracles of Azusa Street and Beyond* (Shippensburg, PA: Destiny Image Publishers, Inc., 2013), 48.

163 Brumback, *Suddenly*, 38-39.

164 Robeck, *Azusa Street Mission and Revival*, 99.

165 Menzies, *Anointed to Serve*, 53-54.

166 Robeck, *Azusa Street Mission and Revival*, 99.

167 "Pentecost Has Come," *The Apostolic Faith*, September 1906, 1.

168 "The Pentecostal Baptism Restored," *The Apostolic Faith*, October 1906, 4.

169 "Bible Pentecost," *The Apostolic Faith*, November 1906, 2.

170 "Bible Pentecost."

171 "Pentecost With Signs Following," *The Apostolic Faith*, December 1906, 1.

172 "Pentecost Both Sides of the Ocean," *The Apostolic Faith*, March 1907, 1.

173 Ibid.

174 "Fires Are Being Kindled," *The Apostolic Faith*, May 1908, 1.

175 Ibid.

176 Menzies, *Anointed to Serve*, 54-55.

177 Brumback, *Suddenly*, 42-43.

178 N4CM, "One-Fourth of Christians 'Speak in Tongues,'" May 2, 2018, accessed September 30, 2021, http://churchandstate.org.uk/2018/05/one-fourth-of-christians-speak-in-tongues/.

Chapter 8: Healing Revivals of the 1920s

179 Brumback, *Suddenly*, 42.

180 Ibid., 256.

181 Brumback, *Suddenly*, 272.

182 David W. Dorries, "The Making of Smith Wigglesworth Part One: The Making of the Man," *Assemblies of God Heritage* (1992): 6.

183 Ibid., 6-7.

184 Ibid., 8.

185 Ibid., 32.

186 Gary B. McGee, *People of the Spirit* (Springfield, MO: Gospel Publishing House, 2004), 208.

187 Joseph S. Girdler and Carolyn Tennant, *Keys to the Apostolic and Prophetic: Embracing the Authentic Avoiding the Bizarre* (Crestwood, KY: Meadow Streams Publishing, 2019), 33-34.

188 Ibid., 40.

189 Dorries, "The Making of Smith Wigglesworth," 28.

190 McGee, *People of the Spirit*, 209.

191 Ron McIntosh, *The Quest for Revival* (Tulsa, OK: Harrison House, 1994), 39.

192 Ibid., 151.

193 Blumhofer, *Assemblies of God: Volume 1*, 249.

194 McIntosh, *Quest for Revival*, 41.

195 McGee, *People of the Spirit*, 151.

196 Blumhofer, *Assemblies of God: Volume 1*, 250.

197 Aimee Semple McPherson, *This Is That* (Los Angeles, CA: Foursquare Publications, 1923), 311–312.

198 Ibid., 324-325.

199 Ibid., 329.

200 McGee, *People of the Spirit*, 152.

201 McIntosh, *The Quest for Revival*, 42.

202 Ibid.

203 Blumhofer, *Assemblies of God: Volume 1*, 251.

204 McGee, *People of the Spirit*, 155.

205 Blumhofer, *Assemblies of God: Volume 1*, 252.

206 Charles S. Price, *The Story of My Life* (Yuma, CO: Jawbone Digital, 2017), 15.

207 Ibid., 24.

208 Edith L. Blumhofer, *Pentecost in My Soul: Explorations in the Meaning of Pentecostal Experience in the Early Assemblies of God* (Springfield, MO: Gospel Publishing House, 1989), 222.

209 McGee, *People of the Spirit*, 304.

210 Price, *The Story of My Life*, 39.

211 Tim Enloe, "Dr. Charles S. Price: His Life, Ministry, and Influence," *Assemblies of God Heritage* (2008): 8.

212 Ibid., 9.

213 Price, *The Story of My Life*, 71-74.

214 Enloe, "Dr. Charles S. Price," 11.

215 McGee, *People of the Spirit*, 305-06.

216 Marjorie Stewart, "A Story of Pentecost in the Pacific Northwest," *Assemblies of God Heritage* (1987): 19.

217 Ibid.

218 Burke, *Like a Prairie Fire*, 84.

219 Betty Tucker, interview by Daniel Tidmore, September 18, 2021.

220 Burke, *Like a Prairie Fire*, 334.

221 Blumhofer, *Restoring the Faith*, 170.

222 Smith Wigglesworth, *Smith Wigglesworth on the Holy Spirit* (New Kensington, PA: Whitaker House, 1999), 10.

223 "Get Ready for 'The Coming Revival—Dr. Charles S. Price's Prediction from 75 Years Ago! | Flower Pentecostal Heritage Center," accessed September 27, 2021, https://ifphc.wordpress.com/2014/07/15/get-ready-for-the-coming-revival-dr-charles-s-prices-prediction-from-75-years-ago/.

224 "History," *The Foursquare Church*, last modified November 10, 2017, accessed September 27, 2021, https://www.foursquare.org/about/history/.

Chapter 9: Hebrides Revival

225 Duncan Campbell, *The Lewis Awakening: Revival in the Hebrides* (Independently Published, 2017), iii.

226 Ibid., vii.

227 "Revival in the Hebrides (1949)," adapted from writings by Duncan Campbell and others (compiled by Jim Meletiou, transcribed from a tape by Duncan Campbell made in 1968), accessed September 24, 2021, https://notjustnotes.webs.com/Hebrides.pdf, 2-3.

228 Daniel K. Norris, *Trail of Fire* (Lake Mary, FL: Charisma House, 2016), 163.
229 "Revival in the Hebrides," 3.
230 Norris, *Trail of Fire*, 163-165.
231 "Revival in the Hebrides," 3.
232 Owen Murphy, *When God Stepped Down from Heaven* (Center Mark Press, Amazon Digital Services, 2012), 16.
233 "Revival in the Hebrides," 304.
234 Norris, *Trail of Fire*, 165.
235 "Revival in the Hebrides," 4.
236 Norris, *Trail of Fire*, 167-168.
237 "Revival in the Hebrides," 5-6.
238 Campbell, *The Lewis Awakening*, 11.
239 "Revival in the Hebrides," 8.
240 Ibid., 10-11.
241 Murphy, *When God Stepped Down*, 27.
242 Duewel, *Revival Fire*, 314.
243 "Revival in the Hebrides," 12-13.
244 Ibid., 22.
245 Ibid., 23.
246 Murphy, *When God Stepped Down*, 31.

Chapter 10: Argentine Revivals

247 Rocky Grams, *In Awe of Argentina* (Lake Mary, FL: Creation House, 2006), 37.
248 Ibid., 32-33.
249 R. Edward Miller, *Secrets of the Argentine Revival* (Peniel Outreach Ministries, Inc., 1999), 1-2.
250 Grams, *In Awe of Argentina*, 34.
251 "Tommy Hicks: El Primer Avivamiento En Argentina Que Alcanzó a Juan Domingo Perón," Enfoque Evangélico, accessed September 22, 2021, https://enfoqueevangelico.com.ar/tommy-hicks-el-primer-avivamiento-en-argentina-que-alcanzo-a-juan-domingo-peron/.
252 Miller, *Secrets of the Argentine Revival*, 61-62.
253 Grams, *In Awe of Argentina*, 35.
254 Miller, *Secrets of the Argentine Revival*, 64-65.
255 Ibid., 68.
256 Grams, *In Awe of Argentina*, 35-36.
257 Miller, *Secrets of the Argentine Revival*, 70-73.

258 Grams, *In Awe of Argentina*, 36.

259 "1984 Argentina Revival," Beautiful Feet, accessed April 25, 2022, https://romans1015.com/1984-argentine-revival/.

260 "The Awesome Argentina Revival," accessed September 22, 2021, https://thestandard.org.uk/the-blog/item/the-awesome-argentina-revival.

261 "1984 Argentina Revival."

262 Grams, *In Awe of Argentina*, 56.

263 Ibid., 53.

264 "1984 Argentina Revival."

265 Grams, *In Awe of Argentina*, 54-55.

266 "The Awesome Argentina Revival."

267 Grams, *In Awe of Argentina*, 64.

268 Ibid., 66.

269 Ibid., 133.

270 Ibid., 140.

271 Ibid., 148.

272 "The Awesome Argentina Revival."